BAD
Teacher

BAD Teacher

Hilarious tales of staff misbehaving

JENNY
CROMPTON

Michael O'Mara Books Limited

First published in Great Britain in 2013 by
Michael O'Mara Books Limited
9 Lion Yard
Tremadoc Road
London SW4 7NQ

A CIP catalogue record for this book is available from the British Library.

Papers used by Michael O'Mara Books Limited are natural, recyclable products
made from wood grown in sustainable forests. The manufacturing processes
conform to the environmental regulations of the country of origin.

978-1-78243-149-7 in paperback print format
978-1-78243-166-4 in ebook format

1 2 3 4 5 6 7 8 9 10

Illustrations by Andrew Pinder
Cover design by Greg Stevenson
Designed and typeset by Envy Design Ltd

Printed and bound by CPI Group (UK) Ltd, Croydon, CR0 4YY

www.mombooks.com

CONTENTS

INTRODUCTION

SCHOOL: the best days of our lives! Or so we are always told. But ask anyone who's a few decades into their post-school life to name some outstanding memories of their formative years and they'll most likely have little or no recollection of the things they were taught but a wealth of vivid stories about the people who actually taught them. If school days really are the best days of our lives (and, let's be honest, the jury's still out) then surely it is our teachers who make them so – occasionally by being so inspirational as to change lives and help fulfil dreams, but more often than not by the moments of random madness that see them talk nonsense, take bewildering mental detours, make awkward personal revelations, send everyone home in tears, devise ill-considered 'interactive' lessons, adhere slavishly to health and safety rules, set the classroom on fire, set themselves on fire …

This catalogue of errors from around the world is a celebration of the wit, wisdom and world-weary bafflement of the teachers we've all loved, and loved to hate. From slips of the tongue to mad, bad and dangerous behaviour, it seems teachers are living proof that, if something can go wrong, it will. (Though that said, and in the immortal words of teachers everywhere, if you think *you're* so clever …)

So quieten down at the back, please, and let's begin.

THE WORM HAS TURNED

DRINK, DRUGS, DISORDERLY CONDUCT…
AND THAT'S JUST THE TEACHER.

Mad Bad and Dangerous to Know

MIDDLE SCHOOL RELIGIOUS studies students in New Haven, Connecticut, USA, were delighted to hear that their teacher was unwell one morning, and justifiably bemused to be greeted by a supply teacher instead. But they soon began to suspect that Ms Bennett's class would be one to remember when she started behaving rather oddly, talking distractedly and gazing up at the sky. When she then singled out all the spectacle-wearers, ripped their glasses from their faces and flung them out of the window, crying 'God needs them to see your love for him, my children!' – their suspicions were confirmed.

AN AGEING maths teacher in Kent, UK, was renowned among her pupils for paying scant attention during class; most lessons involved her setting an hour's worth of calculations and then inventing spurious reasons to go to the staffroom so that she could smoke.

Inevitably her bored students took to devising ever more ludicrous schemes to rouse her from her reveries, and the gauntlet was well and truly thrown down after two of them managed to excuse themselves mid-lesson by announcing they were both due at a Grade 3 banjo exam. Not to be outdone, the class clown climbed onto a windowsill at the back, jumped out onto the grass, walked around the side of the classroom in full view of her incredulous friends and the teacher – had she been looking – and then wandered back in through the classroom door and sat down as if nothing had happened.

Unsurprisingly, nothing happened.

A SPANISH teacher returning from a week's illness was stunned to be rounded on by the colleague who'd covered her classes in her absence. Apparently the teaching paraphernalia on her desk had prevented him from spreading out his newspaper to do the cryptic crossword.

AN ANCIENT French teacher in Warwickshire, England, was either too engrossed in verb declension or simply counting down the days until retirement when he failed repeatedly to stop his bored students from passing the time by engaging in ever more dangerous activities before his very eyes.

'In the end we took to making flame throwers out of deodorant cans and cigarette lighters,' one of them later recalled. 'The old duffer never noticed, even when we started melting each other's bags. The stench was unbearable.'

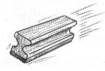

PERHAPS BAFFLED by apparent contradictions in her student-obedience training and her health and safety training, a newly qualified religious studies teacher in London insisted her pupils tidy their classroom, close all the windows, stack their chairs on the desks and then line up in alphabetical order – before adhering to the fire alarm and quickly leaving the building.

STUDENTS AT a small-town Christian school in Texas, USA, were forced to have strange lapses in their knowledge thanks to a devoutly religious teacher who refused to teach anything from page 666 in the textbook. The page was tainted with 'the mark of the beast', she patiently explained, and consequently anything written on it was neither worth knowing nor even looking at.

Q: By what process is water vapour turned into clouds?
A: God.

A PURITANICAL English teacher in Virginia, USA, took her scruples to extremes when misquoted a line from literature in order to avoid saying the word 'breast'. Reading from William Congreve's play *The Mourning Bride*, the teacher said, 'Music has charms to soothe a savage beast.' When a student told her it was not 'beast' but 'breast', he was given detention for using foul language.

A TEACHER in Dublin, Ireland, was infamous among her students for pacing the classroom muttering the instructions for making scones like an incantation: 'Sieve flour, salt, baking powder. Rub in the butter. Add the sugar.' Useful information, certainly, but not entirely relevant to the study of history.

A GEOGRAPHY teacher in Glasgow, Scotland, decided to liven up his class on icebergs with a little role-play. He turned up with a white sheet over his head and spent the entire class in the guise of a talking iceberg.

A CHEMISTRY teacher in Scotland had just mixed two chemicals in a test tube and was holding it up to show the class.

'Now,' he said, 'this is an exothermic reaction, so it can get a little— AAAARGH!'

A WOODWORK teacher in Minnesota, USA, baffled his students when he asked them all to bring their favourite stuffed animal to class the next day. He baffled them even more when he then proceeded to cut off every one of their heads with a rotary saw.

AN ISRAELI teacher tasked with collating a list of troublesome students ahead of a school trip in March 2013 unexpectedly found herself on the receiving end of a stern telling-off when she accidentally emailed the document to the students themselves.

The teacher had polled her colleagues at the Yitzhak Rabin High School in Kfar Saba for frank assessments of their charges and had compiled a spreadsheet in which, for every 'quiet' and 'pleasant' student, there was another who was 'not too bright', who was 'a sicko' or 'a big baby', or who had 'a voice like a four-year-old' or 'a thing for boys'.

The students in question refused to let their teachers brush the incident under the carpet, turning up for school the next day with their supposed flaws taped prominently across their chests and inviting reporters to cover the story.

TEACHING ISN'T known as the most lucrative of careers, and one teacher in Boca Raton, Florida, might in normal circumstances have been forgiven for doing the occasional spot of moonlighting – if only her choice of freelance work had involved her wearing rather more items of clothing.

In April 2013 it emerged that Olivia Sprauer, an English teacher at Martin County High School, had instead taken 'moonlighting' quite literally and been working as an 'eye-candy model' for a magazine run by XXXTremeVisionRadio. Under her assumed identity of Victoria Valentine Jones, she had revealed in an interview that she would be 'more than comfortable shooting tasteful nudes for the right projects'.

The school board generously gave her the opportunity to begin considering the tastefulness of such projects sooner rather than later by firing her on the spot and having her marched off the premises, although Sprauer told reporters she had been planning to make a career move into full-time modelling in any case.

NO MATTER how enthusiastic most new teachers are at the start of their educational odyssey, there sadly comes a time for many when they realize that, when all is said and done, teaching really is just a job – and a thankless, ill-paid one at that. But reveal this apathy to your students at your peril, teachers: nowadays every single student is potentially just seconds away from turning your world-weary rant into an instant Internet sensation.

In May 2013 a certain Mrs Phung, a teacher in Duncanville, Texas, made a throwaway comment in class that implied her interest in world history extended only as far as her next pay slip. Within hours she was notorious the world over thanks to the Oscar-worthy rant of one of her pupils, which had been captured on a mobile phone and uploaded to YouTube.

'You want kids to come into your class?' yells the student, identified only as Jeff. 'You want them to get excited for this? You gotta come in here and make them excited. You want a kid to change and start doing better? You gotta touch his freakin' heart. You gotta take this job serious, this is the future of this nation. And when you come in here, like you did last time, and make a statement, about "Oh, this is my pay check" – indeed it is. But this is my country's future, and my education.'

Mrs Phung's reaction is not recorded, though she may well have decided her next teaching pay cheque ought to be her last.

A LVERPOOL geography teacher who had given forty years of loyal service and was nearing retirement made no great effort to hide her disdain for the political correctness of the modern world. World-weary and, by this stage in her career, approximately as fascinated with plate tectonics as her students were, she droned her way through the syllabus while counting down the minutes.

One particular GCSE class was fairly unique in this teacher's experience for containing two students of Asian origin, neither of whose names she had the patience to commit to memory. One lesson, finding that nobody was willing to answer her question on fault lines, she picked on one of these girls.

'Shonali? What kind of fault line is this, Shonali?'

'Um,' answered the girl, 'I'm not Shonali.'

'Oh, fine,' the teacher snapped impatiently, '"the other one": what kind of fault line is this?'

She was put out to pasture very soon afterwards.

A HISTORY teacher who had evidently got out of bed on the wrong side found himself quite unable to control an unruly class of teenagers later that morning. Things came to a head when he resorted to smashing chairs against the floor in a misguided attempt to gain their attention, and eventually he gave up entirely and stormed out of the classroom – which shut them up at last.

'Sadly,' reports one sheepish student, 'the effect was ruined somewhat when he had to slink back a few minutes later to collect his coat, wallet and keys.'

HEARING AN almighty racket in the neighbouring classroom, a formidable history teacher left her own class working in silence and burst in on the roomful of teenagers talking loudly, sitting on desks, listening to music and throwing various projectiles.

'STOP!' she yelled. 'Where on earth is your teacher?'

There were awkward looks all round when one girl pointed towards a meek-looking creature at the blackboard and said, 'Right there.'

WHAT MOST teachers fear more than bad exam results or unruly pupils is The Sudden Distraction, a momentary incident that incites mass hysteria among the pupils, who then need at least twenty minutes to settle down again. More often than not, such distractions take the form of a creature of some sort flying through an open classroom window, and while some teachers take these crises in their stride – one English teacher in London was interrupted by a startled pigeon, which flew round the room defecating on the screaming students until she quick-wittedly dispatched someone to fetch the swimming-pool net and then fished the bird off one of the rafters – others evidently get caught up in the pupils' infectious panic.

'During class when I was about eight,' recalls a former student, 'I suddenly noticed an enormous wasp was crawling up my bare leg. I screamed, everyone around me screamed and suddenly I was in the middle of the room on my own, everyone else pressed against the walls. The teacher looked terrified but I begged her to help me, so she grabbed the nearest weapon to hand – a can of air-freshener – and sprayed it all over my leg as I sat there screaming. Then all of us watched in stunned silence as the wasp quietly choked in the scent of Summer Meadow and dropped off.'

A FIFTEEN-year-old boy was forced to turn to home education in June 2013 because of incessant bullying at his New York school. His tormentors at the Christian institution took issue with the fact that Noah Kilpatrick was originally Canadian, even though he had lived in the United States for ten years, but what irked the boy most about his mistreatment was that the perpetrators were not his fellow students but rather his teachers.

The school principal was by all accounts particularly fond of bringing up Noah's Canadian heritage, mocking him in front of the whole school for accidentally giving a cafeteria worker a Canadian coin and taking a mental detour during a history class to point out that all Canadians are stupid.

Baffled by this bizarrely specific xenophobia, Noah's mother felt she had no option but to remove him from the school – and perhaps even from the country.

A VETERAN English teacher who was presented with an essay written in an illegibly small scrawl didn't waste time trying to decipher the student's thoughts.

'I'm too old to read this,' she wrote at the top of the paper. 'What grade do you want?'

> Student: Surely the indoctrination of kids into Christianity is akin to brainwashing.
>
> Religion teacher: Nonsense. All the Christians in this classroom: put your hands up if you feel brainwashed.

A TEACHER accused of improper conduct towards one of her students came up with a remarkably brazen self-defence: she was too racist to want to touch a black child.

Police investigating the case reported that Esther Stokes, a prep school teacher in Texas, had told them 'she doesn't like black children because she was prejudiced', and on a more personal level that she simply 'does not like the complainant'.

Unsurprisingly, the teacher was not invited back at the start of the next term.

AFTER A Pennsylvania science teacher allowed a student to indulge in his hobby – body-piercing – during class, she was forced to admit it had been something of a 'lapse of judgement'. The student, who had brought his own piercing kit with him, not only pierced the navel of one of his fellow students but also pierced the teacher's ear.

Q: What practical steps can ecologists take to reduce the amount of litter in rivers?
A: Teach fish to eat rubbish.

STUDENTS AT a school in Massachusetts began to suspect something was amiss with Ms Brady in April 2011 when she began doing chicken impressions in the middle of class and then asked one boy: 'How would it feel to have a bullet in your head?'

Coming to the conclusion that 'something was wrong with her', the children alerted the school

authorities, who alerted the police – who in turn, using their superlative investigative skills, determined that the Gatorade bottle from which Ms Brady had liberally been chugging contained an alarming amount of alcohol.

More remarkable still, neither the school nor parents pressed charges.

A SUMMERTIME bonding session between teachers and parents went slightly awry when, during a light-hearted game of rounders, the chemistry teacher let go of the bat and sent it flying at one unsuspecting mother's head.

After a moment of shocked silence the incident was laughed off as a hilarious accident – until five minutes later when he did the same thing again. For the sake of maintaining good relations the teacher was sent home by the headmaster.

A PROFESSOR of English refused to get out of character during the summer holidays when she had a public meltdown at a Manhattan branch of Starbucks after being told she had not used the correct words to order her lunch. Lynne Rosenthal had ordered a simple bagel in August 2010 but was faced with the inevitable attempted 'upsell' when the barista asked if she wanted butter or cheese with that. Professor Rosenthal repeated her order – one bagel – but this seemingly did not conform to Starbucks' corporate language.

As she reported to the *New York Post*, 'The barista said, "You're not going to get anything unless you say butter or cheese!"' But Professor Rosenthal was having none of it, continuing: 'I refused to say "without butter or cheese". When you go to Burger King, you don't have to list the six things you don't want.'

Even after being manhandled off the premises by

three police officers, Professor Rosenthal stuck to her guns.

'Linguistically, it's stupid,' she said, 'and I'm a stickler for correct English.'

A YEAR 7 girl who'd done a bad job of tying her own school tie one morning made sure to learn the correct method after her irate form tutor barked: 'Good grief, I've seen ants with longer penises than that.'

Illegal Eagles

A WORLD-weary teacher in New York thought nothing of telling her students they had their 'brains in their ass' – until she was hauled before a tribunal, at which point she compounded her troubles by bribing the students to give investigators a positive character assessment for her.

The teacher was particularly keen to get an endorsement from one failing pupil, whom she telephoned five times prior to the hearing in 2012, promising a passing grade the student would otherwise not have attained.

In her defence, the teacher claimed the whole incident had been a 'misunderstanding', though she didn't endear herself to investigators by citing the difficulties of teaching Hispanic children as a reason for her outburst.

A SEVENTY-four-year-old Massachusetts maths teacher saw her long career brought to an abrupt end in 2011 when it emerged that she had been operating a meth lab out of her house.

Irina Kristy and her son had been under police surveillance for a year and were eventually charged with 'distribution of meth, conspiracy to violate the drug law, and drug violation in a school zone' after investigators raided their house and found 'a large amount of materials believed to be hazardous', including a number of items they felt compelled to destroy by controlled detonation.

She is most likely sorely missed by her former students, who fondly remembered her as 'an easy grader'.

IN LATE 2012 a class of California students began noticing things going missing when their bags were left unattended during PE. After accusations and counter-accusations among the classmates proved futile, one of the students decided to resolve the matter through good old-fashioned espionage.

Justine Betti, a fifteen-year-old pupil at Linden High School, somehow tricked her way out of the sports lesson and instead hid in one of the changing-room lockers. What she saw was astonishing: one of the teachers was stealing the students' belongings.

'After all the kids left she stayed in there and went through people's backpacks,' the girl later told reporters. 'I saw her take money. I didn't want to believe that she would do something like that because she was so nice.'

Alas, her classmates being even more incredulous than Justine had been, nobody believed her. The next week she snuck out of gym once again and this time filmed the theft on both her phone and a camera. The evidence was incontrovertible.

Credit to the teacher in question, though: she was so popular among students that even those from whom she had stolen said they 'couldn't help but feel bad for her ... She was a great teacher.'

AN ENGLISH teacher in North Carolina tapped into the teenage craze for unusual recreational drugs in 2012 when she began selling prescription medication on school property. Indeed, so successful was Meredith Burris Pruitt's business venture that she even employed students to sell the drugs on her behalf, pocketing a nice profit in the process.

Apparently without any hint of irony, the *Huffington Post* reported that 'some students were sad to see the teacher leave'.

PERHAPS HOPING to make some extra cash in his spare time, a foolhardy teacher in Emerainville, outside Paris, took to cultivating drugs at home, an endeavour in which he might never have been caught out had he not brought them into school to sell to his pupils.

According to *Le Parisien* newspaper, the twenty-nine-year-old teacher of history and geography would boast to his pupils about regularly taking drugs, before telling them he could fix them up with whatever they might want and outlining his price list. The police were called after the headmaster learned that joints were being sold on school property by a member of his own staff, and a search of the teacher's home uncovered not only cannabis-growing paraphernalia but also magic mushrooms.

In April 2012 the teacher was sentenced to six months in prison and was banned from teaching for five years.

A Drop of the Hard Stuff

AN ELEMENTARY school field trip to a Wisconsin bowling alley ended in unexpected debauchery when one teacher became so drunk that she vomited and passed out, and had to be collected by her husband.

According to reports, the fifty-year-old teacher had a blood alcohol level of .27 by noon – over three times the legal limit. She did not help her cause by admitting to hospital staff that she had started drinking at 6 a.m.

Q: How could you determine the height of a building using a barometer?
A: Lower the barometer off the roof using a really long piece of string. When it touches the ground, measure the string.

Q: What is the highest frequency noise that
the human ear can register?
A: Mariah Carey.

THERE IS little better remedy after a heavy night out
than a 'hair of the dog' drink and a little snooze –
unless it's a school day and you're due in class.

Jill Lyle, a substitute teacher in New Mexico, had
just gone to shut her eyes for a minute or two in
a room adjoining her classroom, but she was
discovered a while later passed out and with a
suspicious-looking beverage beside her.

'The liquid in the cup was red and had an odor of
alcohol,' local Sherlock Holmes Lt Louis Carlos told
reporters. 'We do believe it was a cup containing
wine there with her in the classroom.'

The teacher came to shortly after being whisked
away in an ambulance, no doubt tearfully telling the
medics she loved them very much and had never felt
such a spiritual connection.

TEACHERS ACCOMPANYING a British school orchestra on a performance tour of Prague were left with some explaining to do after one of the girls got so drunk on vodka that she had to be hospitalized and missed her flight home. At least, they reasoned, she had thrown herself into all that the local culture had to offer.

THANKS TO a devil-may-care chemistry teacher from Devon, one group of former pupils remember their first alcoholic drink only too well.

'He was teaching us about ethanol,' one of them fondly recalls, 'and actually let us all take a sip. We were thirteen. The rest of the day was hilarious at first, and then awful. A few years later I bumped into him at a music festival and he gave me a couple of joints, so I can honestly say he taught me everything I know about hazardous chemicals.'

SUPPLY TEACHERS get a rough deal at the best of times but one stand-in at a school in Calais, France, let his frustration get the better of him when he managed to slap three young children during a single lesson. Unsurprisingly the police were summoned, whereupon they determined that the teacher was 'in a drunken state'.

It's a cautionary tale for any supply teachers thinking of making a similarly dramatic exit from a detested school. French news website The Local reported that this teacher was fined, banned from teaching for two years, given a suspended jail sentence and packed off to an alcohol-addiction clinic.

ANYTHING TO DECLARE

TASKED WITH WRITING ENDLESS REPORTS
AND MARKING REAMS OF BOOKS, YOU CAN FORGIVE
TEACHERS FOR OCCASIONALLY VEERING INTO
DANGEROUS TERRITORY: TELLING THE TRUTH.

The Full Report

A DISILLUSIONED YOUNG English teacher in Japan was required every term to write a brief summary of each student's performance, using a formulaic report card that demanded one positive comment, one negative comment, and then a recommendation for the future. Alas, the drudgery of this pointless exercise eventually took its toll on the poor woman's level of diplomacy ...

Positive: High level of communicative ability.
Negative: Looks like a gnome.
Recommendation: Growing pills.

Positive: Admirable grasp of English.
Negative: Stinks.
Recommendation: Dental floss.

Positive: Living and breathing.
Negative: Nonchalant. Shit for brains.
Recommendation: Lobotomy.

ALL TEACHERS claim to hate writing their annual reports, but these real-life examples, vividly recalled by the students in question, suggest otherwise...

'Since my last report, your child has reached rock bottom and has started to dig.'

X

'I would not allow this student to breed.'

✓

'Your child has delusions of adequacy.'

X

'Your son is depriving a village somewhere of an idiot.'

'Your son sets low personal standards and then consistently fails to achieve them.'

✗

'The student has a full six-pack — but lacks the plastic thing to hold it all together.'

✓

'This child has been working with glue too much.'

✗

'When your daughter's IQ reaches 50, she should sell.'

✓

'The wheel is turning, but the hamster is definitely dead.'

✗

'The gates are down, the lights are flashing, but the train isn't coming.'

✓

'If this student were any more stupid, he'd have to be watered twice a week.'

'It's impossible to believe the sperm that created this child beat out 1,000,000 others.'

✗

'This is the work of someone with a mental handicap.'

✓

'This child farts too much.'

✗

'She gets distracted easily ... sometimes by nothing but herself.'

✓

'Popular with peers ... and staff ... Not so much with textbooks.'

✗

'If only she used her pen as much as she uses her mouth ...'

✓

'I'm relieved to see he has received such a good report from his other teachers, because frankly his performance in PE is atrocious.'

'If she stopped falling asleep in lessons and did some more work, I'm sure she could reach the required level.'

X

'The improvement in his handwriting has revealed his inability to spell.'

✓

'Give him the job and he will finish the tools.'

X

'Rugby: Hobbs has useful speed when he runs in the right direction.'

✓

'French is a foreign language to Fowler.'

X

'The stick and carrot must be very much in evidence before this particular donkey decides to exert itself.'

✓

'He has given me a new definition of stoicism: he grins and I bear it.'

'At least his education hasn't gone to his head.'

✗

'Would be lazy but for absence.'

✓

On the annual report of a persistent truant: 'Who?'

✗

'Jane is a born leader – unfortunately she is leading the class in the wrong direction.'

✓

'The tropical forests are safe when John enters the woodwork room, for his projects are small and progress is slow.'

✗

'Henry Ford once said history is bunk. Yours most certainly is.'

✓

'For this pupil all ages are dark.'

✗

'Tamara's performance in physical education is severely limited by lack of speed or coordination.'

'He has an overdeveloped unawareness.'

✗

'This boy does not need a Scripture teacher. He needs a missionary.'

✓

'About as energetic as an absentee miner.'

✗

'Unlike the poor, Graham is seldom with us.'

✓

'He has emitted slight signs of life recently.'

✗

On the report of a child on epilepsy medication: 'I am not always convinced that his stupors are barbiturate-induced.'

✓

'Woodwork but won't.'

✗

'Time not dedicated to self-adornment is devoted to the neglect of his studies.'

'He has contributed much during his time here, some of it helpful.'

✗

'She was consistent throughout the whole school year: she talked and talked and talked and talked and talked.'

✓

'Your son is wasting my time and your money.'

✗

'Hockey: Who is this girl?'

✓

'Geography: Does well to find his way home.'

✗

'Words fail me.'

✓

'The oases of his enlightenment are as nothing compared with the vast deserts of his ignorance.'

✗

'Continues to perform with vigour and enthusiasm on the games field, but will come to realize that his efforts will be better rewarded when applied within the rules of the game.'

X

'If ignorance is bliss, this boy's happiness must be colossal.'

✓

'Displays his ignorance with enthusiasm.'

X

'I expect to be a calmer and less emotional person next year, without your child in my class.'

✓

'Has a one-track mind. It's a pity it's a dirt track.'

X

'Attainment: C. Effort: C. She continues to work to the best of her ability.'

✓

'When the workers of the world unite it would be presumptuous of Dewhurst to include himself among their number.'

'Seems to understand the subject in class discussion; the problems arise when he starts writing.'

✗

'Perhaps when he goes on to read French at university, he will finally realize that French is not English-in-a-French-accent and begin using a dictionary.'

✓

'He might as well not be in the room.'

✗

'Has brains. Fails to use them.'

✓

'He thrives on interaction with his peers.'

✗

'She talks and plays whenever the chance occurs. And whenever it doesn't.'

✓

'This child is a mobile health and safety hazard.'

✗

'High expectations don't intimidate her.'

'Machines, tools and materials tremble in fear when he enters the workshop – and so do I!'

✗

'Works well – when reminded.'

✓

'We fear this boy is doing his best.'

✗

'He has made himself at home here, but really ought to take his feet off the mantelpiece.'

✓

'Music: Hits all the wrong notes with enthusiasm.'

✗

'It is to be hoped that he does well in his exams, because he will certainly not be invited back.'

✓

'Your son has a remarkable ability in gathering needed information from his classmates.'

✗

'Not known at this address.'

'Unmatched in his capacity for blending fact with fiction.'

✗

'Like the Spartans, she is always combing her hair.'

✓

'Pregnant with good intentions, but as yet there is no sign of labour.'

✗

'Having never seen the boy, I cannot form an honest opinion.'

✓

'God, being omnipotent, never made a mistake. But John is the nearest he ever came.'

ONE MOTHER was amused to see evidence of infighting between two teachers on her son's end-of-year report. Under the sports teacher's comment – 'Stuart makes a mockery of the game of cricket' – his maths teacher had scribbled: 'Quite rightly.'

A SCHOOL in Suffolk, presumably spurred on by one too many ill-written missives, was compelled in November 2012 to place an advertisement for a part-time proofreader. The ad on the Northgate High School website highlighted the kind of errors the proofreader was likely to be faced with: 'spelling mistakes, poor or missing punctuation, incorrect capitalization' and 'poor grammar'. The headteacher also envisaged 'extensive correcting by giving them feedback on their report writing and tactfully suggesting strategies to help them improve'.

Q: Name one smoking-related condition.
A: Death.

Marking from the Hip

AFTER TURNING in a woefully inadequate essay and yet still receiving 70 per cent for it, a history student in Sydney began to suspect his teacher hadn't read a word of it. Sure enough, when he loitered near the teacher's desk after class one day, 'I watched as he looked at the first page for a few seconds, then gave a 70 to every single student in class.'

Meanwhile, in Alabama, a seasoned history teacher simply awarded 100 per cent to the students he considered brainy, without going through the tedious formality of actually reading their homework.

'We'd get our fill-in-the-blanks worksheets back and mine would be marked 100 per cent,' one student recalled, 'while the kids who'd copied my homework would be marked down for writing things like: "George Washington lead the <u>Russian</u> Army across <u>Canada</u> in the year <u>1994</u>."'

DURING AN English class about grammar and tenses, Mrs Brown asked her students to complete the sentence: 'If I were Mrs Brown for a day, I would _____.' The general consensus was that this alternative Mrs Brown would bring pizza to class and award everyone an A.

The following day the students arrived to find that Mrs Brown had indeed brought pizza to class.

'It's the least I could do,' she explained. 'Your other request was impossible.'

Influential person in World War 2:
Jimmy McPerson *(Teacher comments in italic)*

Jimmy McPerson isn't a well-sung hero. He isn't in any historybooks, not many people have even heard of him. Some might argue he was never even a documented citizen.

Born to a young African slave couple, Jimmy grew up in Harlem, in up-state Chicago *(Harlem is in New York)*. Like all young black youth, Jimmy joined a gang *(What?)*, in order to get his "props." Times were good.

Until the Japanese performed a sneak attack on young Jimmy's town *(The Japanese never attacked New York OR Chicago)*, killing his parents instantly. Jimmy swore revenge on all the Japanese, and promised to avenge the death of his parents, who were on the verge of curing cancer. Jimmy couldn't join the army *(Yes he could)*, because Martin Luther King Jr. wasn't born yet *(Yes he was)*. So Jimmy had to form a plan.

Using a new name, Jimmy snuck into the Japanese base in Tokyo, and fought off countless samurai and ninjas, until he came face to face with the president of Japan *(Do you mean Emperor?)*. "President Maximoto! Now you're going to pay!" Jimmy said, but little did he know that right behind him was Hitler *(Oh God, no)*. Jimmy fought valiantly, but he was no match for both Hitler and President Japan. With his dying charge, he pushed Hitler out the window, falling with him to his death.

(Very cute, Peter. If Jimmy was forgotten by history, how do you know about him?)

The Perils of the Internet

IN 2011, Pennsylvania teacher Natalie Monroe was suspended after authorities were alerted to her personal — and, sadly, swiftly removed — blog, on which she vented her true feelings about students, parents and colleagues.

In a blog post about the blandly PC report cards she and her colleagues were forced to write, she made a long list of more brutally truthful statements she wanted to see 'added to the canned comment list, as an accurate reflection of what we really want to say to these parents'.

Ms Monroe's best bon-mots:

- 'There's no other way to say this, I hate your kid.'
- 'Although academically OK, your child has no other redeeming qualities.'
- '[Your child is] a complete and utter jerk in all ways.'

- 'I didn't realize one person could have this many problems.'
- 'Two words come to mind: brown AND nose.'
- 'Gimme an A. I. R. H. E. A. D. What's that spell? Your kid!'
- 'Asked too many questions and took too long to ask them. The bell means it's time to leave!'
- 'Lazy asshole.'
- 'Out of control.'
- 'Rat-like.'
- 'Frightfully dim.'
- 'Rude, lazy, disengaged whiners.'
- 'Dresses like a streetwalker.'
- 'Just generally annoying.'
- 'I hear the trash company is hiring.'

'The truth hurts sometimes,' she added. Indeed it does.

A STUDENT in the United States was so incensed at having a test moved forward by one day that he took to Twitter to vent his ire. 'I hate you, Mr Torrence,' the boy wrote. 'You said the test was on Wednesday, so give it to us on Wednesday, not Tuesday. #YouNeedACalendar #ScrewYou'.

Alas Mr Torrence was rather more tech-savvy than the student had bargained for. He not only saw the message on the social networking site but also reverted to old-school classroom technology to exact his revenge. When the student's class arrived for Mr Torrence's next lesson, the incriminating tweet was projected across the front wall of the room.

ONE TEACHER in the United States grasped modern technology by the horns and set up a Facebook page on which he would post homework assignments, useful links and answers to previous tests. By 'liking' the page, however, his students unwittingly also gave him access to every personal update they posted – many of which, it transpired, were about how much they hated this teacher's class.

'My fave,' the teacher wrote on gossip website Gawker.com, 'was the student who posted one night that he hadn't even started my BS project, it was stupid, etc., and he was just going to tell me his printer broke. I commented, "Let me know how that works out for you." He handed in the project the next day.'

OVERSTEPPING THE MARK

SEX, SEX, SEX: IT'S ALL THAT TEENAGERS
CAN THINK ABOUT; AND TEACHERS, TOO,
BY THE LOOKS OF THESE STORIES.

Know your Audience

A P.E. TEACHER in Birmingham finally admitted defeat against Mother Nature one rainy morning and had to come up with an indoor activity on the hoof. She took the class of eight-year-olds to the computer room but there were no DVDs to hand, so she asked them what they were learning about in science. 'The human body,' came the reply. Applauding herself for her admirable cross-curricular initiative, she typed 'human body' into an educational website and hit 'play' on the first video that came up – only to find herself broadcasting an

explicit sex-education film to the room of innocent faces, and subsequently forced to answer some spectacularly awkward questions from the pupils and their bemused parents.

A NURSERY school teacher near Rouen, France, learned the hard way that 'you can't turn your back for five minutes' when she sat her class of three-to five-year-olds down in front of a cartoon she'd downloaded from the Internet and popped out of the room to take a call.

As the traumatized toddlers later reported, what the teacher had assumed was an episode of the child-friendly *Oui-Oui* was in fact a film in which 'people first had clothes on, and then they were naked'.

Returning to the classroom five minutes later, the teacher was horrified to find the children watching hardcore porn and apologized profusely to parents for what the headmaster called 'an extremely regrettable accident', leaving everyone to wonder quietly to themselves how on earth such a mix-up could have occurred.

STUDENTS AT an all-girls' school in Kent dreaded their weekly English lesson once it became clear that their teacher was obsessed with discussing sex. 'She liked to wear miniskirts and tight tops and talk breathily about anything vaguely sexual in the novels we read in class,' one mortified former student remembers. 'On more than one occasion she climbed onto her desk and casually lay on it as she led a discussion about fanciable men in literature. We were eleven.'

IN 1969 an English teacher at a North London Catholic grammar school found himself in the unenviable position of having to cover a chemistry class for a teacher who was off school sick. Having perhaps come a cropper on a previous attempt to impart some useful stand-in knowledge on the topic in question, he decided not to bother winging it this time.

'I know f**k-all about chemistry,' he announced to the children, 'so I have decided to read you an excerpt from *The Little Red Schoolbook*' – a controversial Danish handbook that encouraged students to question authority, with extensive sections on the positive uses of sex and drugs, and which had been banned in the UK under the Obscene Publications Act.

'It was extremely enlightening to many of us naïve souls,' one of the students later recalled in a comments thread on the *Guardian* website. 'How he got away with that I'll never know.'

AN ENGLISH teacher took a class of eleven-year-olds by storm on their first day at a prestigious school in Brighton in the mid-1970s when she marched into the room and announced, without prompt or preliminaries: 'Girls, I have to tell you that Byron takes me to orgasm every time ... I hope he does the same for you.'

'Needless to say,' one of the wide-eyed students recalled many years later, 'she captivated us and set the tone for a very precious year of education.'

A Slip of the Tongue

AS THE only non-elderly male teacher in an all-girls' school, and a teacher of biology at that, Mr B was already the subject of extensive pubescent whispering and giggling by the time he came to be instructing a room full of fourteen-year-olds on evolution and the survival of the fittest. His lesson oft-interrupted by facetious comments (fittest – ha ha), Mr B was caught unawares by the bell. In the scrum to collect all the fossils, bones and other artefacts he had passed round before his students disappeared, he blocked the doorway and yelled: 'Girls! Who's got the horn?'

A SPANISH teacher in London realized it was time for a holiday when, in the course of a single lesson, she told one boy to 'come and shit at the front where I can see you' and, referring to a late piece of homework and the diminutive departmental office, commanded another to 'give it to me in the Spanish cupboard at lunchtime or else'.

'I thought a break-time coffee would sort me out,' she later commented, 'but in the next class, when asked how long the homework essay ought to be, I actually said, "You know me: the longer the better," and the whole class erupted into giggles.'

A PHILOSOPHY class on Utilitarianism – 'the right thing to do is that which causes the greatest happiness' – descended into uncharacteristic chaos when the teacher asked her students to make lists of 'higher' (intellectual) and 'lower' (human) pleasures. Noting that they had omitted eating from the second list, she prompted: 'Can you think of a lower pleasure you haven't got on this list, and it's something you do at least three times a day...?'

DURING A digression about cock-fighting in a lesson about medieval pastimes, one teacher asked her first-year class: 'Does anyone know another word for a cock?'

Answers were fulsome and plentiful.

ONE FRENCH teacher made a memorable impression on her new A-Level class during the first lesson after the summer holidays. Morale was low and the room was stifling, and the boys were becoming increasingly distracted while she explained important exam information to them. In exasperation she eventually exclaimed, 'Look. You're hot, I'm hot – let's just get on with it, OK?' They were all ears after that.

A BIOLOGY teacher in Dietrich, Idaho, was hauled before the school board after parents complained that he had used sexually explicit language in front of their children – during his classes on the reproductive system.

Tim McDaniel had forewarned his teenage students that the topic would be appearing on the syllabus and that they need not attend if they felt uncomfortable with the material, but not a single pupil had opted out. Their parents, however, were outraged to discover that McDaniel had not only mentioned STDs, birth control and orgasms but had also taught the students about climate change and uttered the word 'vagina'.

'I teach straight out of the textbook,' the harassed teacher told reporters in March 2013 as he awaited the conclusions of a formal investigation into his 'inappropriate' lessons. 'I don't include anything that the textbook doesn't mention.'

A spokesman from the Idaho State Department of Education suggested McDaniel would get away with a stern rap on the knuckles, and presumably a newfound wariness of scientific facts.

A GEOGRAPHY teacher was lecturing her class about ocean currents, regaling them with facts about the Coriolis effect, wind direction, thermohaline circulation ... Lots of big words, but she spoke slowly and patiently as the children took notes: 'Ocean currents flowing away from the equator are called warm currents,' she explained. 'The water in these currents is not necessarily warm, but it's warm compared to what you would expect for that latitude. The Gulf Stream is a good example of a warm ocean cunt. Any questions?'

One polite girl put her hand up: 'Um, did you just say the big C-word?'

AN ART teacher in Hampstead, London, was left red-faced when showing her class of young boys how to fashion a miniature Stonehenge out of clay. Having brought one of the boys to the front of the class to demonstrate the construction of a perfect prehistoric megalith, she had him roll out a crossbeam for the top, which they put aside while they dealt with the vertical columns. Once the standing stones were actually standing and it was time to add the crossbeam, she said, with a flourish, 'Now, for the final touch, let's show everyone your little sausage…'

Should Have Known Better

IN MOST places of work there is little wrong in a harmless office romance, but an affair between school employees on school premises is another matter entirely… and when students at the Scholars

Academy in Arizona became convinced in 2012 that their principal was up to something with his secretary, they would stop at nothing to find out once and for all.

It was not long before a video emerged, recorded on one student's hidden phone, of the married colleagues locked in what the *Huffington Post* called a 'make-out and groping session' on the school grounds. Faced with the evidence, the principal fell on his sword and resigned, while the secretary was told she needn't return either.

A TEACHER whose work–life balance was evidently weighted at the 'life' end of the scale got her comeuppance when a local news station came across her incredibly revealing Twitter account.

In the guise of @CarlyCrunkBear, an account that was swiftly deleted, Denver maths teacher Carly McKinney not only referred repeatedly to her love of mind-altering substances – 'Nothings better than medical marijuana' – but also tweeted photos of herself enjoying them, alongside photos of her daringly located tattoo, her nearly nude aerobic exercises and a 'goodnight' photo in which she was lying in bed naked. She revealed that a 'jailbait' student had called her 'Ms McCutie', that she was 'stoned' after work, and suggested 'Maybe someday I'll teach high just to see what happens!'

Although McKinney told investigators a friend had posted all the tweets without her knowledge, school authorities remained unconvinced and placed her on administrative leave.

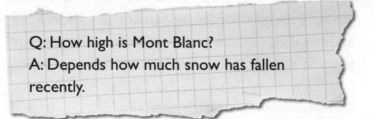

Q: How high is Mont Blanc?
A: Depends how much snow has fallen recently.

FORGOING THE usual awkward euphemisms and embarrassing 1970s educational films, a sex education teacher in New Mexico cut straight to the chase in 2004 by encouraging his students to taste flavoured condoms. A girl who refused was told to 'have a little fun', while a boy who commented, by the by, that he was heterosexual was told: 'Never say never.'

Interestingly, a spokesperson from the New Mexico Health Department defended the teacher's unorthodox approach, saying it was all part of an attempt to 'destigmatize condoms'.

Pupils from a school in York, speaking on condition of anonymity, revealed that their most memorable school trip was the one to Greece during which their matronly biology teacher was spotted cavorting in the ocean with the coach driver.

A FEW generations of students at an all-girls' school in London were forced to endure weekly history lessons with an unnervingly twitchy male teacher who started every lesson by inviting them to 'sit down on those nooks and crannies'. He was only sacked after approaching a pupil at a Central London nightclub and offering her a lift home.

'The following year we walked past him on our way to a hockey match,' remembered one student. 'He was sunbathing in the park in Speedos.'

History teacher: Actually, the Great Wall of China was built to keep people in.
Student: What? Why would they do that?
Teacher: Who knows? It's a Communist government.

STUDENTS AT a school in London were astonished in 2011 to come across a trailer for a pornographic film whose star bore a remarkable resemblance to their teacher. Upon further investigation – purely to establish the facts, of course – they determined that 'Johnny Anglais' was indeed none other than Mr Garrett, head of health education.

After the students reported their discovery to teachers, it emerged that the X-rated movie was not a one-off. Garrett was found to have a website on which he posed in – and out of – a variety of uniforms and costumes, an explicit sexual advice page on Facebook, and a part-time job as a stripper and 'naked butler'. He had also appeared in a trailer for an adult channel called Television X.

'I admit the evidence against me is pretty compelling…' Mr Garrett commented to the press following his suspension from teaching, '… if you believe that pornography is wrong.'

GET YOUR FACTS STRAIGHT

STUDENTS SHOULD BE ABLE TO RELY ON
THEIR TEACHERS TO KNOW THEIR STUFF…
SADLY THAT ISN'T ALWAYS THE CASE, AS
THESE TALES WILL ATTEST.

GEOGRAPHY TEACHER: Canada and the United States are part of the continent of North America. Mexico and the smaller countries south of it are part of the continent of Central America.

Student: But … there is no continent of Central America. Mexico is a North American nation.

Teacher: No, it isn't. Be quiet.

Student: But … I know this is wrong. Look – it says so right here.

Teacher: Ugh, fine. Whatever. You're right. It's not like it matters.

Teacher: Someone give me a controversial issue happening today.
Student: Euthanasia.
Teacher: Good! [writes on blackboard: 'Youth in Asia'].

A BIOLOGY teacher informed her class that they would be dissecting fish the next day, and that she would provide them with specimens she had caught herself. True to her word, she brought a number of dead fish in plastic bags and handed them out to each pair of students.

'When we opened the bags,' one later recalled, 'it turns out she had brought fish that had been cleaned and boiled. Not much knowledge about fish anatomy was acquired that day.'

Student: Miss? Why does 'flammable' mean the same as 'inflammable'?
Chemistry teacher: Um... It doesn't?

THE MIRROR was turned on a sex education teacher who found herself learning a lesson in zoology from her students. She had casually mentioned that cows don't need to have had a calf to be able to give milk. 'They come made like that,' she explained, 'for the purpose of supplying humans with dairy.'

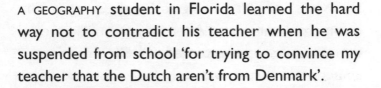

A GEOGRAPHY student in Florida learned the hard way not to contradict his teacher when he was suspended from school 'for trying to convince my teacher that the Dutch aren't from Denmark'.

STUDENT: Sir, what's the Rosetta Stone?
Teacher: Well, I think … I think it's a crystal ball, of sorts.

MATHS teacher: What's seven minus nine?
Student: Minus two.
Teacher: Wrong. It's impossible to subtract nine from seven. It was a trick question.

PARENTS IN South Carolina were bemused in April 2013 to discover their children's lessons on the dinosaurs had a distinctly Creationist slant.

One father, initially delighted that his daughter had got 100 per cent and an A+ on a science test but then alarmed when he read the 'correct' answers, told reporters at Gawker.com: 'I didn't know that this was being taught to her until we heard a radio commercial together about the "Discover the Dinosaurs" exhibit coming to South Carolina. The commercial starts out: "After sixty-five million years, the dinosaurs have returned..." She commented immediately that it was only four thousand years ago. When I corrected her, she snapped back, "Were you there?"'

Genesis, the Creationist organization that had provided the school's science department with its teaching materials, stood by its 'biblical approach to dinosaurs', pointing out that parents had chosen the school for its Christian ethos.

Those dubious test answers in full:

4TH GRADE SCIENCE QUIZ
DINOSAURS: GENESIS AND THE GOSPEL

1. True or false? The earth is billions of years old. FALSE
2. True or false? Dinosaurs lived millions of years ago. FALSE

3. On what day did God make dinosaurs?
   6TH

4. True or false? Dinosaurs lived with people.
   TRUE

5. Which of these fits the Behemoth
   mentioned in Job 40: elephant,
   rhinoceros or dinosaur?
   DINOSAUR

6. Whom should we always trust?
   GOD

7. What is the 'History Book of the Universe'?
   THE BIBLE

8. The average size of a dinosaur
   was equivalent to: a giraffe, a
   rhino, an elephant or a sheep?
   SHEEP

9. What caused there to be fossils: lightning,
   a Global Flood, a tornado or evolution?
   GLOBAL FLOOD

10. Fossils are …?
    BILLIONS OF DEAD THINGS BURIED IN
    ROCK LAYERS BY WATER

11. The next time someone says
    the earth is billions (or millions)
    of years old, what can you say?
    WERE YOU THERE?

AN ENGLISH teacher in Boston was convinced she had caught a serial plagiarizer when she came across the word 'zeitgeist' in an essay. Demonstrating a woeful lack of faith in her own standard of teaching, she had assumed the boy 'was too stupid to know what it meant'. She presumably began scouring the jobs pages of the newspaper after another pupil in the same class had to prove to her, by showing her the dictionary entry, that 'ergo' was a valid word in English.

'She thought I had just made the word up,' the accused student recalled. 'But she was forced to admit that I knew of, and could correctly use, words that she didn't know existed.'

Meanwhile, in Melbourne, a student was upbraided for using the 'invented' word 'ruffian' in an essay. The teacher refused to believe the student when he protested that he had looked the word up in the dictionary to double-check his spelling, saying he was far too young to know how to do that.

A SUBSTITUTE teacher called in to cover an IT lesson in the early 1990s was so baffled by a student clicking open the 'options' panel that she sent him directly to the headmaster for presumed 'computer hacking'.

Elsewhere an IT teacher discovered her computer mouse wasn't working and burst into tears – until one bright-spark student pointed out that it wasn't plugged in.

Student: If no one created God, where did he
come from?
Priest: God is like a circle. See, God is like this
circle I'm drawing here: no start or end, it just
goes around and around.
Student: But ... you just put your chalk down
on the board to start drawing that circle. It does
have a start – right there.
Priest: ...

WHEN ASKED by a student what the word 'wanton'
meant, after it appeared in a novel his class was
reading, one English teacher was completely stumped.

'Wanton,' he said with authority. 'As in: I ordered a
bowl of wantons at the Chinese restaurant.'

A VIOLIN player in a school orchestra in Belfast was left more baffled than berated after she tuned her instrument before the teacher had given her permission to do so.

'I was checking to see if my violin was in tune,' she remembers. 'I had only played a couple of notes before the teacher yelled at me: "HAVE I GIVEN YOU PERMISSION TO PLAY? DID I?!" I can honestly say I was speechless.'

THERE WERE awkward looks all round in a physics lesson in Brighton when the teacher wrote the word 'earth' as 'erf' on the blackboard …

AN ENGLISH teacher in London displayed an alarming grasp of the English language while marking an essay in which the student mentioned a character 'crying wolf'. The teacher circled the expression in red ink and scrawled beside it: 'He never said that.'

A TEN-year-old boy in Toronto who had written a story about an old woman with rheumatism was alarmed to be accused in front of his whole class of having copied it out of a book. The teacher was adamant, however, that there was simply no way he could have heard of the condition.

Elsewhere a young boy who had submitted a short story to the school magazine had the piece returned by the editor, his English teacher, because '"chortled" isn't a word'.

A SCIENCE teacher was delighted to be able to teach her class about weather phenomena using an artefact she had found on her way to work.

'She held up this piece of "hail" that had amazingly not melted at all since she had picked it up in the morning,' recalls one unimpressed student. 'It was a white rock.'

A HISTORY student in Ottawa was bemused to find his teacher had not only crossed through the word 'exude' in an essay and replaced it with 'exhume' but then also commented in the margin that '"exhume" is not the correct word to have used in this context'.

PARENTS OF a six-year-old boy began to suspect the school they had chosen was not quite up to scratch when he informed them one evening that he'd had to tell his teacher that veal didn't come from sheep.

A SPANISH teacher in London demonstrated a dubious grasp of cause and effect when she an-nounced to her class the reason Seville is hot is 'because it's close to Africa' – 'as if Africa,' one student commented, 'is some magical heat source'.

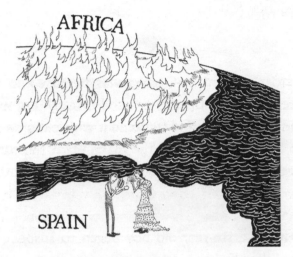

A TEN-year-old boy was left scratching his head after his teacher told him the smallest possible number in the world was 0.01.

'I tried to argue that there could be an infinite number of zeros before the one,' he recalls, 'but my ten-year-old's vocabulary wasn't quite up to the task. She told me I didn't understand and should stop interrupting.'

Teacher: If you laid out your small intestines, they would be long enough to wrap around the earth.
Student: But that means our food would have to be travelling at least at Mach 5 in order for us to digest as fast as we do.
Teacher: It does.

A SMALL school in Ohio evidently didn't see the point in updating its teaching materials after the fall of European communism in the late 1980s and early 1990s. Twenty years later it still insisted students learn the names of obsolete countries including East Germany, West Germany, the USSR and Czechoslovakia – the latter in particular because it was 'easier to remember' than bothering with both the Czech Republic *and* Slovakia.

HAVING PERHAPS based her learning on the lyrics of Alanis Morrissette, an English teacher in Cambridge was renowned for her constant misuse of the word 'ironic', on one occasion telling her class it was ironic that she had lived in a city that was mentioned in their novel – the real irony, of course, being that an English teacher had no idea how to use the word 'irony'.

IN A class about distance and measurement, a science teacher unhelpfully wrote on the blackboard that 1,000 kilometres = 100 metres = 10 metres = 1 metre = 0.1 centimetres = 0.01 centimetres = 0.001 millimetres. When one astute lad tried pointing out that none of those measurements were equivalent to one other, he was told to stop interrupting.

AN IMPATIENT primary school teacher in Surrey deducted marks from one little boy's homework because he had spelled his own name incorrectly, informing the child that he would continue to deduct points until he learned how to spell it. It took a visit from the boy's mother, birth certificate in hand, to convince the teacher that the name was indeed correctly spelled.

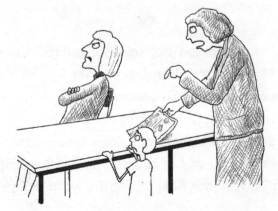

A CHEMISTRY student who tried to correct a teacher's mistake must have wished he had never bothered after they stumbled chaotically from one muddle to the next. Having been politely informed that she was mistaken to say a kilometre is longer than a mile, the teacher looked it up in an encyclopedia and proudly announced: 'Aha, you see! I WAS RIGHT! It says here that a kilometre is point-six-two of a mile!' The child then had to teach her how decimals work.

Teacher: ... and this is an example of an antidote.
Student: Don't you meant anecdote?
Teacher: No, it's pronounced antidote.
Student: No, it isn't. They're two completely different words.
Teacher: Look it up in the dictionary.
Student: OK here, see? It's anecdote.
Teacher: I've been to college, so I'm right.

BAD TEACHER

ALEX'S PARENTS were bemused and worried when he came home from school one day with a note from his teacher, but on reading the letter they had to wonder whether it was Alex or Mr Hilliker who was in need of a stern talking-to:

Dear Mrs X

You may already know this, but in case Alex has neglected to tell you, I am assigning him to detention for one hour this Friday. The reason is as follows: Alex consistently defied me. During class he contradicted me numerous times when I insisted that the length of one kilometer was greater than that of one mile. Every other student in class accepted my lesson without argument, but your son refused to believe what I told him, offering such rebuttals as, 'You're lying to the class', and commanding other students to challenge my curriculum.

Although he was correct, Alex's actions show a blatant disregard for authority, and complete lack of respect for his school. In the future, Alex would be better off simply accepting my teachings without resistance.

Please see to it that your son understands this.

Regards
Adam Hilliker

Q: What sort of work would an Ancient
Egyptian slave have done?
A: Whatever his boss told him.

A BIOLOGY teacher in Minnesota was lecturing his students on health and nutrition.

'People live healthier lives in Africa than in the Western world,' he began, 'because of their healthy lifestyle. They avoid becoming fat and getting cancer, unlike Americans and Europeans. Just look at their statistics: they are not dying of heart-related problems or cancer.'

Hesitantly, one pupil put his hand up and said, as politely as possible, 'Um ... but what if you compared the statistics for death from famine, war and AIDS?'

The teacher moved swiftly on.

HOPING TO spice up a notoriously dull English class, all thirty students tore page 183 out of the novel they were supposed to be reading. The result was that 'pro-' from the end of page 182 was followed at the top of the next page by '-vance'. One mischievous student innocently put her hand up and asked the teacher what 'provance' meant.

The teacher hesitated momentarily before gathering his wits.

'Provance,' he wrote on the blackboard. 'To strive forward hopefully.'

AN ENGLISH teacher reading aloud from *The Diary of Anne Frank* found herself in the unconventional position of having to ask her students the meaning of a word.

'We were celebrating Chanukah,' she read, and then interrupted herself: 'Cha-noo-ka? I'm not sure what this Cha-noo-ka is, but maybe like a birthday or something?'

AN ENGLISH teacher with other things on her mind caused great confusion in a Shakespeare lesson when, instead of talking about 'Macbeth's tragic flaw', she asked pupils to consider his 'tragic whore'.

'What?' asked one girl. 'I must have missed that bit. Does Lady Macbeth sleep with Macduff?'

Teacher: To throw a baseball really far, you need to throw it at a forty-five-degree angle.
Student: Is that forty-five degrees Fahrenheit or Celsius?
Teacher: Er ... Fahrenheit.
Students: [hysterical laughter]
Teacher: Ha ha, I was only joking. It's Celsius.

FOR ALL their assurances to the contrary, even teachers don't know everything. Pay them too much heed and you could well end up with a very skewed understanding of the world around us – as these alternative facts and figures, all of them shared by students on an online forum, indicate.

History

'The Crusades was a war between the Christians and the Catholics.'

✗

'No, the Cold War was before World War II. That's how we developed atomic bombs.'

✓

'I think Pearl Harbor was in World War I. I'm not sure, though, because I'm not a history buff.'

✗

'The South didn't *really* lose the Civil War.'

✓

'The Holocaust killed close to one million people. Your textbook says more than six million but that's just propaganda used at the Nuremberg Trials.'

✗

The day after 9/11: 'Class, this is the start of World War 4.'

✓

'Internment camps in the war were basically big summer camps.'

'The United States invaded Europe in 1944 and then, after they'd won, went to war with Japan.'

X

'The Protestant Reformation was started by Dr Martin Luther King.'

✓

'All the years before AD 1 go backwards because the Egyptians counted backwards.'

X

'It's lucky they never tested an H-bomb – the force might have knocked the earth out of its orbit.'

✓

'Men wear ties because they symbolically cut off the head and point at the penis, thus reinforcing their intellectual dominance over women. This concept was developed by Descartes in the twelfth century.'

X

'The Pyramids were built by aliens.'

'Sputnik was launched by the United States. It contained a monkey.'

✗

'Don't ask me any questions about this. I only just learned it myself.'

✓

'What? Ben Franklin was not a US president? But then why is he on the hundred-dollar bill?'

✗

'People were shorter in the olden days. Abraham Lincoln was only four feet tall.'

✓

'Wikipedia is like porn, which is just as dangerous as heroin.'

✗

Science

'Rocks grow. That's why you see big rocks in the middle of nowhere all by themselves.'

✓

'Hummingbirds don't have legs. That's why they have to fly around all the time, eating.'

'Bats are birds.'

✗

'Seals only eat fish. They're herbivores.'

✓

'Hares are a kind of cat.'

✗

'Black holes don't exist. Don't listen to scientists.'

✓

'The moon is bigger than the earth.'

✗

'The reason you sometimes get that falling sensation before you go to sleep is because it's called *falling* asleep.'

✓

'No, Vitamin D does *not* come from the Sun. It comes from pharmacies.'

✗

'Astronauts need heavy boots to walk on the moon, since there's no gravity. After they walk around to the bottom of the moon they need to take their boots off and then bounce back up to the top.'

'Not all facts are true.'

✗

'Can you read your twin's mind?'

✓

'The kidney is kidney-shaped.'

✗

'Dew is a miracle from God. It can't be explained by science.'

✓

'Of course water is flammable – I just said it was made of hydrogen and oxygen, didn't I?'

✗

'If you stood on the moon and looked at Earth with a telescope you'd see cavemen.'

✓

'The axle of a car's wheel makes more revolutions than the tyre.'

✗

'The hot stuff inside volcanoes is plasma.'

'Gold is a better conductor than copper, which is why the wiring in computers is all made of gold, and that's why they're so expensive.'

✗

'If a smoker suddenly stops smoking they will die.'

✓

'Ships tend to travel southward, because of gravity.'

✗

'When a female chicken lays her last egg, she becomes a rooster.'

✓

'Thunder is a complete mystery. Nobody knows what causes it.'

✗

'Thunder occurs when clouds bump into each other.'

✓

'If evolution is real, why don't monkeys give birth to humans today?'

'Isaac Newton invented gravity.'

✗

'Sorry, I'm just really terrible at explaining things.'

✓

Geography

'You know that saying "All roads lead to Rome"? We have that in the US, too. All roads lead to Washington – except a few that lead out so the President can escape if he needs to.'

✗

'People who live in Europe have purple skin.'

✓

'Greenland is a continent. Europe isn't.'

✗

'Don't be ridiculous – Antarctica has too much snow and ice to be a desert.'

✓

Maths

'There's no such thing as negative numbers.'

'No, thirteen divided by four is not three-point-two-five. It's three remainder one.'

X

'One divided by zero is a really, really big number. There's a huge computer somewhere trying to work it out.'

✓

'Nought-point-twelve is four times larger than nought-point-three.'

X

'You have a fifty per cent chance of winning the lottery. Either you win, or you lose.'

✓

'Your answer is right but you didn't use the right method to get there, so I'm still marking it wrong.'

X

'Zero point five is less than zero.'

✓

'A cube has four sides.'

'A kilometre is longer than a mile because a metre is longer than a foot – and there are a thousand of them.'

✗

'If you extend them far enough, parallel lines will eventually meet.'

✓

'There are three hundred and fifty-six days in a year.'

✗

'Yes, fine: one half and two-fourths and three-sixths are all the same, but you haven't learned how to do that yet so I'm not giving you any points. The answer is six-twelfths.'

✓

'Stop asking why – it's just maths magic.'

✗

'I am not here to amuse you or keep you interested.

I am here to make you suffer. How else will you remember anything if you don't suffer?'

✗

'You're doing this too well. Slow down and stay in pace with the rest of the class.'

✓

English

'Nonplussed? What's that supposed to mean? Coming from you it must be bad – get out of my class.'

✗

'If you're referring to a person, you should use the word "who", not "that". For example: "The man *who* gave me the balloon is kind." This is a very important concept and there are people in this class that are still making this mistake.'

✓

'You have to be pretty stupid to fail your English exam. Basically all you have to do is read the books and somewhat pay attention and you'll be OK.'

'The word "computer" is an acronym for "Commonly Operated Machine Powering on the Unit To get Error-less Result". Memorize it.'

✗

'English and Spanish are so similar because they're both derived from Latin.'

✓

'"B-L-U-E" is pronounced "blu-ee". There's an "e" at the end of it.'

✗

'The plural of "moose" is "meese".'

✓

'"It's" is possessive. "Its" is short for "It is".'

✗

'The word "connoisseur" means the same thing as "amateur".'

✓

'An example of onomatopoeia would be: Saddam Hussein called World War I the mother of all war.'

'*Twilight* is a much better story than the Nativity.'

✗

Politics

'You have no civil rights until you turn eighteen.'
'What are you talking about? Mexico doesn't have
a president. They have a king or an emperor or
something like that.'

✓

'Obama is equivalent to Adolf Hitler and is starting
a communism.'

✗

'It doesn't matter – it's not in the curriculum.'

A HEADMISTRESS in Lincolnshire was forced to make a
personal apology to one set of parents in December
2010 after their daughter's teacher sent them an
email with spelling mistakes and grammatical errors.

In an email whose subject line was 'form tutor
report for parents everning', the teacher gave the
pupil in question a woeful 88 per cent 'attendence'

rate and went on to make more than ten further errors in her message:

I am sorry I was unable to meet with you at the parents' everning this year. However I have enclosed the following for you information

X has ad a hard year but seems to be pulling back onto the right tracks. The end of last year X was quite argumentative on occaisions and even boardering on disrespectful at times however she has settled back down and is now a good role modal for the current year 7's and 8's. X's' uniform is always well present (as is her work) and she is polite when talking to her peers and the staff.

X's attenance is low but some of that can be attributed to her course requriements.

I would personally like to see X taking a more positive role in classroom ativities.

Whether this form tutor also happened to be an English teacher is not recorded.

EXTREME
MEASURES

A TWELVE-YEAR-OLD student in New York who was caught doodling on her desk felt the full force of the law – quite literally being dragged away in handcuffs by the police.

Alexa Gonzalez had scribbled the offensive graffiti – 'I love my friends Faith and Abby' – in erasable ink during a Spanish class in February 2010. When the teacher saw this she marched Alexa to the dean, who called the police, who in turn put the girl in handcuffs and arrested her.

City authorities acknowledged afterwards that they had exercised poor judgement in the incident and Alexa was only subjected to a few hours' community service; she, on the other hand, sued them for $1 million in damages.

CAREER DAY at a school in New Mexico took a turn for the worse when a police officer fired his Taser at a ten-year-old boy. To gain insight into the life of a police officer, the cop had apparently asked the class whether they wanted to wash his car. When one child vocally refused to do so, Officer Webb said, 'Let me show you what happens to people who do not listen to the police' and stunned him with 50,000 volts of electricity.

Needless to say, the rest of the class decided at once to become police officers when they grow up.

A SCHOOL secretary in Pennsylvania caused widespread panic across the county in 2013 when she misunderstood a student's voicemail message and thought he had set off on a shooting spree. The student in question had recorded his own message – a rendition of the theme-tune rap for 1990s TV show *The Fresh Prince of Bel-Air* – which innocently references 'shooting some b-ball outside of the school'. But the secretary, hearing 'shooting some people outside of the school', called the police, who put all the local schools on lockdown while they went on a manhunt.

Pupil: Can I go to the toilet?
Teacher: I don't know – can you?
Pupil: Ugh. May I go to the toilet?
Teacher: What's the magic word?
Pupil: Abracadabra.

IN ONE of the more bizarre cases of overreaction by school authorities, a little boy in Baltimore was suspended after he nibbled his Pop-Tart into a gun shape and said 'Bang bang'. The seven-year-old – who wisely pointed out that 'it kind of looked like a gun but it wasn't' – was suspended for 'using food to make an inappropriate gesture'.

A MISSISSIPPI school caused outrage and hit international headlines in 2010 when it refused to let gay student Constance McMillen bring her girlfriend to the prom. But what is less well known is the bizarre series of events that followed the ill-considered ban.

Having initially cancelled the prom after being told they could not exclude gay couples, organizers were forced by public pressure to lighten up. But what the Missouri school in fact did was send Constance and her girlfriend to a 'fake prom' at a country club, while the rest of the class attended the real event at a location that had been kept secret by teachers, parents and all the other students.

'They had two proms and I was only invited to one of them,' Constance told journalists. 'The one that I went to had seven people there, and everyone went to the other one I wasn't invited to.'

In a bizarre twist that is arguably even more un-PC, the school also dispatched two students with learning difficulties to the fake prom rather than invite them along to the official function.

YOUNG LUCY'S parents were horrified to be called in for a parent-teacher conference with her gym instructor and the headmistress. The reason? She couldn't skip.

A FIVE-year-old boy who got stuck in a 20-foot tree was left there by his teachers because the school's health and safety code instructed them not to help him.

It was only after he had been perched on the high branch for forty-five minutes that a kindly pedestrian who happened to be passing the school's playground came to his aid. The teachers, meanwhile, having consulted their health and safety guidelines, were obediently 'observing from a distance' so that the child would not become 'distracted' and fall.

When the Good Samaritan marched over to the assistant headteacher and reported what she felt was a serious case of negligence, he told her that she was being verbally aggressive – and, moreover, trespassing on school property.

A TEACHER in Narbonne, southern France, demonstrated some impressive self-defence skills when she managed to tie a volatile adversary to a chair. Unfortunately the mother of the three-year-old boy in question had more liberal-minded ideas about what constituted appropriate punishment at a nursery school.

'She tied my son to his chair even as he was begging her, in tears, not to do it,' the mother told local newspaper *Le Dauphiné Libéré*, going on to say that her son had perhaps been 'a little agitated' but had not done anything to deserve such treatment. 'It only lasted a minute or two but that's a very long time for a child.'

The teacher claimed only to have threatened the child with punishment, although it was her word against that of a herd of excitable infants.

WHEN THE governors of a failing primary school in London were forced to bring in a new headteacher one Wednesday morning in February 2011, in an attempt to turn the place around, they little expected to have to sack him before the end of the week. But Craig Tunstall, a so-called 'super-head' on a £200,000 salary, made himself a great number of enemies among parents and teachers alike when he went on an expulsion spree and excluded seven pupils in just two days.

Having insisted that the pupils – some of them as young as five – walk only with their hands behind their backs, Mr Tunstall went on to suspend or expel seven students for offences such as failure to finish lunch, failure to stand in line quickly enough, and failure to wear the correct coat.

'It became clear the arrangement would not work,' said a red-faced spokesman.

EXAM
FAIL

STUDENTS WILL TRY any ruse to avoid answering test questions they don't understand, but in recent years 'the large elephant' has become something of a phenomenon. It essentially involves the student drawing an elephant in the space normally reserved for an answer and writing: 'I couldn't answer this question because an elephant was blocking it.'

One American maths teacher had been faced with this problem enough times to be able to spot a shoddily drawn elephant a mile off. The mark he gave one such chancer was −3. The reason? 'Elephants have tails.'

PUPILS AT a school in Suffolk were bemused in May 2013 to be told two weeks before their A-Level English exam that their teacher had been teaching them the wrong text.

'Our teacher came in and seemed unusually nice and chirpy,' reported one horrified student, 'and then she dropped the bombshell.'

Although there are admittedly parallels between Bram Stoker's *Dracula* and Mary Shelley's *Frankenstein*, exam board AQA had sadly not focused on them in its *Frankenstein*-inspired questions. Having studied *Dracula* for eight months, the students were forced to get up to speed on *Frankenstein* with a five-hour intensive teaching session.

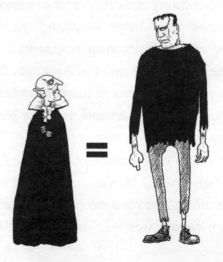

Q: Name an environmental side effect of burning fossil fuels.
A: Fire.

A STUDENT in Scotland had the exam experience from hell when her physics teacher, invigilating the physics exam, picked up her paper mid-exam 'and started chuckling as he read it'.

AN ELEMENTARY school in Brooklyn sought to incentivize its teachers to achieve higher test results for students by offering the teachers a priceless reward: smaller classes and fewer non-English-speaking pupils. It seemed a fair deal and results at Public School 94 did indeed take a miraculous turn for the better – until it emerged that certain teachers, desperate not to fail, had routinely been handing out the answers to tests.

Q: Give a brief explanation of the meaning of the term 'hard water'.
A: Ice

TIRED OF watching his students stare longingly at the classroom clock during lessons, a science teacher in California displayed a message for them where he knew they couldn't miss it. In large letters above the clock was written: 'TIME WILL PASS'. And beneath it: 'WILL YOU?'

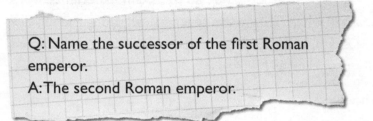

Q: Name the successor of the first Roman emperor.
A: The second Roman emperor.

AN ANONYMOUS teacher who had reached the end of his tether with a class so awful that it was known within the French department as 'The Somme' – as a columnist for the *Times Educational Supplement* reported in July 2011, 'the kids were not allowed pencils or pens for fear they would stab each other' – was reduced to teaching his students French swear words in return for them paying attention. The system seemed to work tolerably well until the day one boy suggested, in French, that the headmaster might like to perform an explicit sex act.

Asked to explain how the boy had come to learn such colourful language, the teacher feared an instant dismissal. Instead, he reported, 'the head was so impressed boy X had learned something, he's promoting me next year.'

Q: What do we call a person who is forced to leave their home, perhaps by war or natural disaster, without another home to go to?
A: Homeless.

Q: A pair of spectacles are dropped from the top of a 32.0m high stadium. A pen is dropped 2.0s later. Draw a dinosaur wearing spectacles and holding a pen. (Disregard air resistance, $g = 9.81 m/s^2$.)
(YOU MUST SHOW YOUR WORK TO GET CREDIT FOR THIS PROBLEM.)

TEACHER: THIS piece of paper is the size of one gram.
Student: One gram of what?
Teacher: I'm not taking questions.

Q: Brian is driving at 40 feet per second in a 40mph zone. Is he speeding?
A: Brian can easily find out by looking at the speedometer.

Q: Calculate the difference between 1,937 and 4,001.
A: No.

Invigilation Olympics

EVERYONE DREADS the summer exams – but none more so, it would seem, than the qualified teachers forced to spend excruciating hours, weeks, even years, silently invigilating the wretched things.

'If you think that doing an exam is boring, as someone doing an exam,' former PE teacher Mike Bubbins told BBC Radio 4 listeners in May 2013, 'then watching someone do an exam is ten times as boring.'

With a flagrant disregard for the good behaviour they are trained to insist on, teachers have over the years come up with ingenious ways to stave off mind-numbing boredom, transforming the tedious exam season into a season of high-octane

Invigilation Olympics. Forget hockey, netball and rugby: these sports are guaranteed to have even the most lethargic of players begging to be picked first.

Pacman

The challenger surreptitiously approaches another teacher and whispers 'Tag' in their ear, before turning on his heel and calmly walking away. The target must count slowly to five before following the challenger in a demented zig-zag of the exam desks. Strictly no running, and only ninety-degree turns allowed.

Stand by Me

Another daring tag-team event in which one teacher challenges another to – in the words of Mike Bubbins – 'stand by the child who's likely to be a father first', 'the girl likely to be a grandmother youngest', 'the chap most likely to fail all his GCSEs', 'the boy most likely to be on the front of a newspaper later in life'. With potential targets as varied as the ugliest child and the one most likely to wind up in prison – or, as a number of university examiners have admitted under condition of anonymity, 'the student I would most like to…' – this sport mercifully provides hours of entertainment.

Get to the Point

Two teachers, two sharpeners, two piles of blunt pencils. Race!

Copycat

Taking inspiration from the noble art of step aerobics, this sport involves the teacher at the front of the exam hall performing a series of subtle stretches and shoulder exercises – which, unbeknownst to the students, are being copied in a highly exaggerated manner by all the other teachers standing at the back.

Good Kid/Bad Kid

Teacher A selects a pupil whom Teacher B does not know, and it is Teacher B's task to study the student and guess at his or her intelligence, behaviour and level of personal hygiene.

Battleships

Based on the popular naval-warfare game, the invigilation edition is played using desks as 'squares'. Having drawn the exam-hall layout on two sheets of paper, the players select the locations of their 'battleships' and then 'launch missiles' using secret hand signals across the room – or, for the more daring, by demarcating the desks they have targeted on foot.

The Race

A simple one, this, but arguably one of the most dangerous, given the need for speed and the potential for catastrophic collision. Armed with paper, tissues, pencil sharpeners and cups of water, the teachers position themselves around the exam hall, scouring the sea of heads for any signs of movement. Suddenly Sally Jones in seat 19D puts her hand up – and it's a race against time, and one another, for the teachers to attend to her every need. The teacher who has handed out the most sheets of paper at the end of the exam wins.

The 100-Metre Sprint

In the final race of the Invigilation Olympics, the champion is the teacher who can beat all others at collecting the exam papers from his or her row.

Individual Games

When exam-hall team sports are thwarted by fellow invigilators' slavish adherence to the task at hand – after all, as a killjoy at the Qualifications and Curriculum Authority insisted when questioned by the *Times Educational Supplement* in 2004, 'Teachers are supposed to be focusing on the behaviour of pupils and what's going on in the exam room' – there is still hope for individual competitors. Indeed, comments posted on the *TES* website and the BBC News website reveal the extraordinary lengths some teachers will go to to mark the passage of time:

- Read the graffiti on each desk as you pass by.
- Translate the exam paper into foreign languages.
- Make figures out of Blu-Tack, with extra points for producing an uncanny likeness of the nearest student.
- Practise belly-dancing routines.
- Calculate the length of the floorboards used to floor the exam room.
- Calculate the height of a column that could be made from the bricks that make the walls.
- Count the shuttlecocks trapped in the sports hall lights, and then the distance they travelled to get there. Physics teachers should also have a stab at their likely velocity.

- Count the number of students wearing glasses, divide this by the number of redheads in the hall and add the number of coughs in a ten-minute period. Expert players report that, if the number of children with visible nits is subtracted, the answer will always be four.

A SAN Francisco teacher whose class was heading towards certain failure came up with a novel way of motivating them to exam success. Stanley Richards promised his students that, if they could raise

City Arts and Technology High School's academic performance by fifty points in the summer of 2011, he would tattoo his calf with an image of the vice principal dressed as a sumo wrestler, slaying a dragon.

They did. He did.

'I was ninety-nine per cent sure it wouldn't happen,' the newly inked science teacher told *The Bay Citizen* newspaper.

A MUSIC teacher in Angus, Scotland, was suspended in March 2013 after it emerged that he had substituted his students' coursework compositions with pieces

he himself had written, and then submitted them to the exam board without the students' knowledge. In all, nineteen students had their work secretly upgraded by the veteran composer, who admitted all charges of 'acting dishonestly' in a misguided attempt to ensure the highest grades.

Just one year earlier another teacher in Scotland was struck off for writing English literature essays on his students' behalf. The ruse came to light when an examiner realized the suspiciously insightful essays discussed poems the candidates had never even studied.

THE EXAM season of summer 2011 proved particularly tricky for AS-Level maths students in 335 schools across the United Kingdom when, in what exam board OCR called an 'unfortunate error', they were set a question that was literally impossible to answer.

An estimated 6,800 students were faced with the unanswerable problem, which was worth eight of the paper's seventy-two points, asking them to calculate the shortest route for a series of journeys whose distances simply didn't add up.

'I spent a good fifteen minutes trying to answer

that question,' one frustrated student told BBC News. 'I can't believe how much time was wasted on a question where we were only able to get zero marks.' Another said that 'the exam was hard enough without an impossible question making it even harder', while a third student demonstrated a sound understanding of the subject at hand by commenting that 'eight marks is over ten per cent of the paper'.

Despite the excellent suggestion made by one commenter on the BBC News website – 'Just ignore the question and mark the paper out of sixty-four; it's basic maths, not rocket science' – OCR refused to discount the question entirely in its marking but graciously offered to take into account students' valiant attempts to find a non-existent answer.

Teacher: The universe is expanding and the stars are flying further apart. Imagine rising dough with raisins in it.
Student: So what does the 'dough' consist of?
Teacher: Oh, it's just regular cookie dough.

THE EXAM season can be as stressful for teachers as it is for their pupils; with grades proving the efficacy (or otherwise) of a whole year's teaching, reputations are very much on the line.

How mortifying, then, for one primary school teacher in England who looked through her eleven-year-olds' exam scripts in June 2010 and found that eighteen out of nineteen of them had got one of the questions wrong. So desperate was she to see them succeed that she changed their answer before sending the papers to the exam board. Alas, she was quickly caught out – not only because the new answer was clearly written using a different pencil, but also because it was completely incorrect.

A LITERATURE teacher in Maine gave a frank assessment of one student's prospects by stapling a job application form for Burger King to her failed test.

A PHYSICS teacher who'd evidently seen far too many students pulling the 'massive margins' trick to make an essay seem longer than it is decided the time had come to take action. In the margin of one particularly underwhelming effort, the teacher had carefully measured the width of the margin, noted down the exact measurement, and deducted 5% from the student's score.

A HISTORY student who thought he'd take a shortcut to the perfect essay by seeking help on an Internet forum got an unexpected response – from his own teacher.

Faced with a complex question he couldn't quite be bothered to answer, the student headed straight to Yahoo Answers and posted the title of his essay: 'To what extent did social tensions escalate and divisions among Americans deepen in the 1960s?' Adding his own personal touch to the end of his appeal for help, he continued: 'like with the civil rights movement and vietnam and hippies. lol, but is that right with civil rights and the vietnam war?'

The response, which received a 100% approval rating from other Yahoo Answers users, was: 'Yes. Tensions between academic cheaters and their teachers escalated in the 1960s. They have remained high to this day, especially when savvy professors browse Yahoo Answers the night before papers are due and look for the questions they assigned. See you in class tomorrow!'

A HISTORY teacher who had to take a day off school when her students were due to take a test asked the stand-in teacher to project a slide she had prepared on the front wall of the classroom. Next to a photo of the teacher cheerfully marking papers were the words: 'Hello, everybody! Unfortunately, I cannot be here today, so here is a picture of me looking professorial instead.'

FOLLOWING AN exam in which some students were let down by woefully under-length essays, one teacher in America sent his class some helpful advice by email:

'A good rule of thumb for essays is called the "mini-skirt rule" — they should be long enough to cover what needs to be covered and short enough to be interesting. For many of you, your essays were more comparable to an "elderly, overweight man in a Speedo" — your essays were way too short, didn't cover much at all, and some were just sad and pathetic.'

ADVICE

A T AN ALL-GIRLS' school in Surrey a male English
teacher took a detour from a discussion of
Pride and Prejudice to inform his students that
they would have to 'dumb it down' if they had any
intention of marrying, 'because men hate smart
women'. He then suggested they spend less time
preparing for lessons and more time learning how
to cook and clean.

A STUDENT who had relocated to a school in
Mississippi had a useful lesson on the local dialect
during her first English class when the teacher spent

quite some time explaining the difference between 'y'all and 'all y'all'. Apparently the cut-off point for 'y'all' is seven people.

CONVINCED THAT 'girls aren't good at maths', an irascible teacher in Leeds would pick on the females in his class to answer tricky questions. When they inevitably got it wrong, he would shake his head sadly, choose a boy to attempt an answer and then bellow, 'YES! *He* got it right!'

Q: Give an example of an animal that can't move.
A: Dead cat.

DURING A lesson about the Holocaust, a teacher with a limited knowledge of the subject made a number of statements that sticklers might have considered spectacularly incorrect. Eventually a Jewish pupil stood up and told her that her understanding of Jewish culture was abysmal. In time-honoured tradition, she snapped, 'Well, if you know so much about it, why don't you come up here and teach the class yourself?'

He did.

As one student later recalled, 'He was funny as sh*t. The teacher sulked in the corner.'

Q: What is sexual bullying (give an example)?
A: Punching someone in the vagina.

TEACHER: ?? Who in their right mind would do this? A class on the civil rights movement drifted into awkward territory when the teacher told his pupils to use marker pens and paint to colour their hands and faces – so that they could 'feel what it's like to be black'.

EXPERIMENTAL
TEACHING

A CHEMISTRY TEACHER in London donned lab glasses and thick gloves and told his class to prepare for something spectacular.

In increasing horror they watched as he plunged his hand into a flask of liquid nitrogen, then pulled it out and smashed it to pieces with a hammer. Blood and petrified flesh spattered onto his lab coat and over half the front row. One girl fainted.

When the headmistress was summoned to calm the room of hysterical children, the teacher was forced to concede that a ketchup-filled glove was perhaps an inappropriate teaching tool.

A MATHS teacher in Washington, DC, no doubt thought he could inspire his students to take an interest in the notoriously tedious subject by setting them calculations based on computer-game-style scenarios. Unfortunately the problems, featuring death, disease and cannibalism, proved a little too much for his eight-year-old class.

The school principal was bemused at the maths teacher's 'bad judgement', clarifying in a statement that the questions had been downloaded from the Internet rather than taken from the officially sanctioned textbook.

Some of the more nightmarish sums from the rogue paper:

1. Green aliens landed in Chicago and rounded up 1479 math teachers. The bloodthirsty aliens then sucked the blood of 828 teachers and left them for dead. The aliens tied up the rest of the teachers and marched them into 3 UFOs. If there were an equal number of poor math teachers in each UFO, how many teachers were in each UFO?

2. My 3 friends and I were caught and tied up by 1023 screaming cannibals in a jungle last night. Soon we were feeling terribly itchy because

of the mosquitoes. We begged the cannibals to scratch us. 219 cannibals refused because they were busy cutting vegetables. The rest of them, however, surrounded us in equal numbers and began to scratch us with their teeth, just like dogs. It felt good! How many cannibals scratched me?

3. John's father gave him 1359 marbles on his birthday. John swallowed 585 marbles and died. 9 of John's friends came for his funeral the next day. John's grieving father gave the remaining marbles to John's friends in equal numbers. How many marbles did each friend get?

4. My brother and sister kept 263 trolls in a huge cage in our backyard. They went into the jungle yesterday and caught more trolls. When they came back home, they brought back 8 sacks and 7 boxes. There were 8 crying trolls in each sack and 7 shrieking trolls in each box. They threw the trolls into the cage with the other trolls. How many trolls are in the cage now?

5. Brian, a brave member of a SWAT team in California, had a terribly busy week last week. He had to work for 7 whole days. He killed 163 terrorists, 296 murderers and 206 arsonists. How many criminals did he kill on average each day?

6. Tilda Tiger had many hungry children to feed on Thanksgiving Day. She caught 169 Africans, 526 Americans and 196 Indians. She then put the people equally into 9 enormous ovens to bake. How many desperate people were in each oven?

7. When I was sleeping in a forest last night, 2555 fire ants crawled up my nose and built a nest in my brain. I woke up screaming the next morning. My distraught mother rushed me to hospital for an emergency operation. The doctor was able to kill 1953 fire ants. The remaining ants in my brain formed themselves into 7 equal-sized groups and fled to 7 different organs in my body, one being my stomach.

- a) How many fire ants escaped?
- b) How many ants fled to my stomach?

Q: Give appropriate names for these triangles.
A: Sarah, Alan, Stuart.

Teachers at an English-language school in Brazil hit upon a novel way of encouraging their students to be passionate about good spelling and grammar. Having noticed the appalling state of most celebrities' tweets, the teachers at the Red Balloon School set their pupils the task of scouring Twitter for badly executed celebrity missives and replying to the A-list stars with helpful grammar corrections.

While some might question the educational benefit in asking children to read the ill-written ramblings of the rich and famous, the Red Balloon teachers defended their unconventional curriculum, saying they wanted the children to understand that they shouldn't emulate the kind of English they found online.

A selection of @redballoonBR's best responses:

@DanielRadcliffe: Hello guys, It have been an age that I didn't tweet , thanks all for your amaizing messages. DAN XX
@redballoonBR: Dear Harry Potter, I'm Gabriel, from Brazil. Your tweet has 2 mistakes: "it has been" and "amazing".

@KimKardashian: Up early getting ready to film Chelsea Lately today with the whole fam! Were taking over tonight!!!

@redballoonBR: You're beautiful. I'm Ana Beatriz from Brazil, I'm 8. Look, you wrote Were, but it's "we're". Kisses.

@rihanna: She's my rock so I hold on to she tight!!!

@redballoonBR: Hi! I love your songs. My name is Carolina. I'm 11 years old. It's not to she, it's to her.

@MileyCyrus: So many peeps I love birrrfday is today!

@redballoonBR: Hi, my name is Amanda and I'm a big fan from Brazil. Look, "birthday" has no Fs :)

@souljaboy: She not a queen if she don't belong to a king

@redballoonBR: Mayara and Ana from Brazil here. We're 11 and 8 years old. Did you mean "she's not" and "she doesn't"?

@justinbieber: Some video games. Some old movies … That was a long bus ride. But we here.

@redballonBR: Hi! My name is Maria, I'm 9 and I'm a fan from Brazil. Watch out: it's "we're here" not "we here" :)

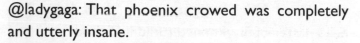

@ladygaga: That phoenix crowed was completely and utterly insane.

@redballonBR: I'm Milena, 10 years old from Brazil. You're great but your tweet has a mistake: crowd doesn't have an "e".

@charliesheen: short break from the kooky part of my brane

@redballonBR: I'm Rafael from Brazil. Big fan. But man, use your "brain", not your "brane" :)

A SCHOOL in Worcestershire raised eyebrows among parents and police officers alike when it staged the violent gangland murder of a teacher in front of his whole class.

The incident, which had been designed as a fun exercise in crime-scene investigation, took the children by surprise and left many of them in tears over Mr Kent's seemingly dead body. The headmaster of Blackminster Middle School admitted that 'the acting was a bit too enthusiastic', although he expressed regret that the teacher chosen to play dead had been one of the most popular.

'I don't think there would have been as much concern if it was one or two of the others.'

ONE CHEMISTRY teacher left a memorable impression regarding the flammability of potassium when a flaming lump of it fell to the floor during class. Reassuring the students that there was nothing to worry about, he stamped on it briskly, set his shoe alight and prompted a mass evacuation of the whole school.

Q: How does Romeo die?
A: On the *Titanic*.

EXPERIMENTAL TEACHING

A CHEMISTRY teacher in Manchester adopted a novel approach to engaging his new class with the traditionally tedious subject.

Mr Kyle seemed to have got off to a terrible start by showing up fifteen minutes late; the students were sitting on the tables or wandering about, talking loudly and listening to music. Without a word he wandered over towards the blackboard, produced a match and set his desk on fire. In open-mouthed silence the students watched the flames spell out 'Kyle is cool'.

Then he extinguished the blaze and began his lecture on the subject of ethyl alcohol.

IN MAY 2013, after UK Education Secretary Michael Gove criticized a history teacher who had encouraged students to create a 'Mr Men' character based on Adolf Hitler, the *Guardian* website asked its readers to post their own examples of unconventional teaching methods, many of which painted an ... unusual picture of British education standards:

- 'My history teacher introduced the subject of the political parties of Weimar Germany through a "speed-dating" exercise.'
- 'For my A-Level English we had a section on monsters, containing excerpts from *Frankenstein*, *Dracula* ... and then *Pokémon* and *Fungus the Bogeyman*. We were eighteen.'
- 'During an A-Level sociology class, our teacher shut himself in the cupboard for most of the term and demanded we teach ourselves, just to see how difficult it is.'
- 'We were told to research the entire Tudor family tree to a one-hour endless loop of the *Mission: Impossible* theme tune.'
- 'For a poetry lesson one autumn our English teacher made our whole class hold on to a long piece of rope, venture out into the school grounds and see which various items of flora

we could collect from around us without ever letting go of the rope. Then we came back inside and read poetry. I don't ever recall there being an explanation for our "trip" or any reference to what we had managed to collect.'

- 'We watched *Monty Python's Life of Brian* to learn about the Romans.'
- 'My A-Level physics teacher once shot an air rifle into a model train to demonstrate momentum. He wasn't supposed to do it, apparently, but it was "the best example he could think of".'

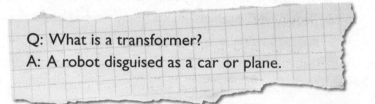

Q: What is a transformer?
A: A robot disguised as a car or plane.

A CLASS of eleven-year-old pupils were left more traumatized than usual following their weekly maths lesson after the teacher inexplicably sidelined fractions and decimals in favour of the horror film *Saw*.

'This will be your first horror film,' the teacher announced to his charges at Collège Jean-Baptiste Clément on the outskirts of Paris, according to

French radio station Europe 1, before flicking on the notoriously gruesome movie in which two strangers find themselves chained in a cellar with a dead body and a series of instructions on how to kill one another or themselves.

After one father, whose young son was 'visibly in some discomfort' and 'not well' when he arrived home that evening, launched a complaint, the school was forced to discipline the teacher – and presumably review its maths curriculum.

Q: Why are there rings on Saturn?
A: Because God liked it, so he put a ring on it.
Teacher: Saturn was <u>NOT</u> a single lady.

Student: I don't understand why you've made this correction in my story.
English teacher: Because we don't say 'black', we say 'African American'.
Student: But ... 'He got into his African American car'?

IN A vivid example of best-laid plans going horribly wrong, Sussex junior school teachers hoping to inspire pupils' creativity by staging an exciting performance were left answering furious questions after traumatizing the children with their supposed 'alien invasion'.

Assembly one morning in 2009 was interrupted by flashing lights and loud sirens, and then the headmistress announced to the 370 pupils at Southway Junior School that a spaceship had crash-landed outside. The bewildered children followed the trail of carefully staged debris to the UFO, whereupon one of their teachers was set upon and abducted by the aliens. Then the children were sent back to their classrooms for lessons.

'God only knows what the school was playing at,' said one teacher of the performance, for which Sussex Police had generously provided props and sirens, and which sent many of the youngsters home in 'a state of shock'.

PARENTS OF twelve-year-old pupils at Collège Louis-Bouland in Couloisy, northern France, were bemused to discover their children's homework assignment one gloomy winter's evening was to compose a suicide note.

As *Le Parisien* newspaper reported in February 2013, the writing task presented the students with the tale of how a man named Jean had come to believe death was the only option and a description of the aftermath of his suicide, before asking them to 'Devise the letter Jean wrote to his wife before carrying out his plan.'

The school stood by its dubious decision but one father echoed the thoughts of all the parents involved when he concluded: 'It's absurd!'

Around the same time, at Collège Montmoreau-Saint-Cybard over in western France, a teacher faced outrage from parents of her thirteen-year-old pupils after she asked them to imagine they were suicidal and to 'explain your reasons at the last minute. Drawing a self-portrait, you will describe your self-disgust. Your text will go over the events in your life that created this feeling.'

The teacher was suspended following a letter from parents in which they asked what on earth might be next on the agenda: 'How do you feel when you shoot up?'

AN ENGLISH teacher in Virginia presumably thought she was getting into the spirit of things by asking one of her students to read out a poem in the voice of the narrator, but it did not look good that her chosen reader of Langston Hughes's 'Ballad of the Landlord' – a poem about a black tenant being jailed in the 1940s – was the only black student in class – and that she criticized him for not sounding black enough.

Interrupting the boy with her director's critique, the teacher supposedly told him to read it 'blacker'. 'I thought you were black,' she added, before giving up and reading the poem herself, in a manner described by the student as 'like a slave, basically'.

In time-honoured tradition, when the student challenged the teacher and asked if she thought that was what all black people sounded like, he was told to sit down and stop speaking out of turn.

Q: How can we prevent milk from going off?
A: Keep it inside the cow.

ON A spurious excuse for a socioeconomic investigation, two geography teachers in Kent took their
class of twelve-year-old grammar-school boys to the
local housing estate to observe the privations of
poverty.

Travelling in convoy in two minivans, both of them
prominently emblazoned with the school's name,
the teachers steered their wary charges through the
narrow lanes of the housing estate, enthusiastically
pointing out signs of impoverishment, and at one
point being chased by two children wielding golf
clubs. Beating a hastier retreat than planned, one of
the teachers managed to get the first van wedged
between two bollards and all thirty students were

forced to stand on the street corner in their pristine school uniform while she performed an eighteen-point turn to extricate the vehicle.

'At least the school's name was partially scraped off by the bollards,' one student recalled twenty years later, 'but the worst bit was when one of our classmates pointed up at the block of flats and glumly said, "That's my house." It was the most ill-conceived educational trip ever. We stopped to eat our packed lunches in a supermarket car park before heading back to school.'

AN INNOVATIVE way to pass the time was adopted by a teacher in Manchester, who would silently throw bits of Blu-Tack at his pupils as they completed whatever task he had set them.

'On one memorable occasion,' recalled a student, 'the teacher made himself an impressive pair of Blu-Tack glasses and wore them for the rest of the class.'

Q: Having read through the case study, can you suggest why Cardiff is not the best location for Sheila's new clothing business?
A: People from Wales are not very fashionable.

ANYONE FORCED to endure them holds a special place in their heart for the weekly music lesson: the scales, the tunelessness, the lack of practice – and, if these stories are anything to go by, the dubious teaching methods of most of the world's music teachers…

- 'My piano teacher was a weird old man with dyed-black hair and a whole load of cats with names like My Little Soldier and The Old Girl. As I would shakily go through my memory of what I had done in the previous lesson – not having touched a piano in the intervening week – the cats would wander along the top of the piano, sit beside me on the bench, or sometimes just sashay along the keys that I wasn't playing. On one occasion, My Little Soldier started climbing up the living room curtains and my teacher leapt to his feet in an absolute rage, spitting insults at the animal's insolence. He climbed onto his chair so as to reach the curtain rail, but his foot went through the bench and we both fell to the floor.'

- 'My violin lessons as a teenager were the best part of my week. I'd be dropped off by my mum, who'd use the lesson time to do her weekly shopping, and then sent to the living room by my teacher to watch old Westerns with her husband while she rustled up some chicken nuggets and chips, and Coke, which I wasn't allowed to drink at home. When we'd finished eating we'd go into the other room and play duets for five minutes before my mum arrived to pick me up. To this day I'm not sure if she was paying my teacher for musical instruction or for babysitting me while she went to the supermarket.'

- 'At school we were taught music by this ancient old battle-axe who'd seen it all and wasn't impressed. We were all terrified of her. Music lessons generally consisted of playing the recorder, surely the most untuneful instrument ever invented, but what we actually spent most of our time doing was applying industrial-strength bleach to the mouthpieces to make them vaguely sanitary.

The school hadn't replaced its recorders in
at least twenty years, you see, so the teacher
would hand out cotton wool and bottles
of bleach and teach us how to disinfect
the spit-filled instruments. Then we were
supposed to put them in our mouths and
play. Unsurprisingly, it's quite hard to play the
recorder without letting it touch your lips.'

A FORMIDABLE professor of Old English grammar was
feared and admired in equal measure by her first-year
university students, who she insisted come for lessons
in her grand home rather than at the faculty so that
she could smoke while teaching. Dodgy translations
were customarily returned to the students with
exclamations of 'Eala!' – 'Alas!' in Old English – scrawled
in the margins, or drawings of the teacher weeping
tears into a bucket, but by far her most notorious trait
was her old-fashioned sense of hospitality.

'Would you like a drink?' she asked two freshers as
they arrived for their first 10 a.m. lesson.

'A cup of tea would be lovely, thanks,' they answered
gratefully.

'No, girls,' she said, her eyes closed in impatience. 'I
said, would you like a *drink*?'

'We didn't learn much grammar that year,' one of the students later recalled, 'but we were entirely sloshed by noon every Monday.'

Q: Why is the birth rate so high in third world countries?
A: They have nothing else to do.

WHEN A student asked if she could open the classroom window one summer's day at a school in Wales, the teacher assented and asked the girl next to her to 'give Sally a hand'. Cue a slow round of applause from the smart Alec, while Sally struggled single-handedly with the window.

There's always one…

Q: Chloe is collecting data about how much junk food her classmates eat. Write down a useful question she could ask them.
A: 'How much junk food do you eat?'

MEDICAL STUDENTS in Taiwan were given a unique perspective on the all-important difference between life and death in 2010 when their professor made them write a will, dress in funeral garb, climb into a coffin and be buried under the floorboards.

'Although it's just ten minutes, the effect is equal to real death,' said the professor at the Rende Medical Centre, going on to explain that the exercise was designed to instil an appreciation of the value of life.

Q: Justin Bieber is thrown horizontally at 10.0m/s from the top of a cliff 122.5m high.
- How long does it take him to reach the ground?
- What is the horizontal displacement?
- What is Justin's final velocity?

HEADTEACHERS! HAVE you run out of inspiration for yet another well-thought-out assembly? Fear not: with these handy tips and pointers – all of them real-life incidents – you need never be lost for words.

Say something so baffling it must be profound:

- Play 'Yellow' by Coldplay and sagely conclude: 'Because you are *all* yellow.'
- Liken a war memorial to a Sunday roast.
- Liken loving God to buying a carpet.
- Declare that the two scourges of the modern world are bald men and pedestrians.
- Prove that 'the sky is not the limit' by unleashing a jar of fleas.
- Enlist three teachers to take it in turns brushing their teeth and swilling their mouths with a single toothbrush and glass of water. As a grand finale, down the entire glass of toothpaste spittle. Declare that this proves Jesus's love for us.

Make bold use of props:

- Smash a load of china with a hammer, bellowing: 'This, children, is what happens to your talent when you don't use it!'

- Demonstrate the importance of tidiness by throwing toast all over the stage.
- Demonstrate the importance of tidiness by throwing sanitary towels all over the stage.
- Demonstrate the importance of tidiness by presenting a gruesome slideshow of photos of the girls' toilets.
- Demonstrate the importance of tidiness by bringing a huge pile of litter on stage and picking out individual banana skins, cigarette butts, etc, yelling: 'Is this yours? IS THIS YOURS?'
- Shame students' disrespect for school property by staggering on stage with a kicked-in cupboard door on your back, like a modern-day Christ en route to the Crucifixion.
- Turn the assembly into a hard-hitting debate show by taking a microphone into the crowd and asking off-the-cuff questions about issues of the day: 'Do you think women should work?', 'Would you say you're a racist?'
- Motivate your students by making them write down something they can't do. Place all the papers in a coffin, solemnly lead the funeral cortege outside and bury 'I can't' in a huge hole dug by the caretakers.

Create a diversion:

- Arrive on stage on a Harley Davidson. Crash and break both legs.
- Tell a long-winded joke whose punchline involves a man being lifted up by his testicles.
- Tell a long-winded story about the time you tweaked Diana Ross's nipples.
- Launch into an off-key medley of Abba songs.
- Come on stage in drag, singing 'Big Spender'.
- Do a risqué dance routine to 'Dancing Queen'.
- Read out a list of your favourite words, including 'diarrhoea'.
- Read out names from the phone book.
- Lead everyone outside 'to watch the mighty Concorde fly past'. Run through the crowd doing an aeroplane impression. Lead everyone back inside.
- Wear a school uniform.
- Wear a gorilla suit.
- Wear a pink tutu and a feather boa.
- Wear an ill-fitting leather jacket and your wife's sunglasses and hammer out a 'cool' song on the piano.
- Bring lambs on stage. Offer no explanation.
- Eat an entire daffodil. Offer no explanation.

- Arrive drunk and bellow 'MARXISM!' End of assembly.

Traumatize them into submission:

- Release an overexcited guide dog into a hall of nervous infants.
- Parade three students as traitors for having quit the school choir.
- Invite a one-eyed explorer to explain to the children how his other eye was pecked out by birds in Africa.
- Be graphic about the Easter story: 'Jesus was nailed through the wrists, not the hands, otherwise the nails would just have ripped through his flesh and he'd have fallen off.'
- Proudly show off the infants' handcrafted models of Tudor monasteries before tearing them all to pieces, as a vivid demonstration of the anguish caused by Henry VIII's destruction of Catholic religious institutions.
- Gravely announce: 'The cybermen are back.'
- Illustrate the dangers of drink-driving by dragging a real, blood-covered body bag onto the stage.

Make awkward personal revelations:

- Confess that you love nothing more than keying other people's cars.
- Regale the children with that time you ran over a family of grouse because you'd assumed they'd fly out of the way.
- Sing a song about your recently deceased dog and then burst into tears.
- Present a slideshow of photos of your child in the bath.
- Describe how you had to administer a suppository to your daughter before leaving for work.
- Describe how your son swallowed a tiddlywink and you had to sift through his poo with a fork to make sure it had come out.
- On the first day back in January give a blow-by-blow account of your 'loneliest New Year's Eve ever'.
- Give a lecture about that crazy acid trip in a caravan in Romania.
- Devote an entire assembly to the colour of your new car (orange).
- Announce that you know from personal experience that there's no need for anyone to use excessive toilet paper. One sheet for a wee; two for a poo.

Homework: please do one of the following by Tuesday:

1. Master Kung Fu.
2. Switch religions for a day.
3. Wear a fake mustache for 24 hours.
4. End world hunger.
5. Find your nemesis, earn their trust, then vanquish them (preferably with magic).
6. In the shower, use conditioner first then shampoo just to see what would happen (I'm curious).

Q: Yo momma's so fat that objects 5 metres away accelerate at 1 m/s^2 toward her. What is yo momma's mass if G = 6.67x10^{-11} Nm^2/kg^2?

AN ASTRONOMY teacher in Ohio found a particularly dispiriting way of reminding his students of their place in the vast expanse of the universe. At the front of the classroom he hung a poster of the Milky Way, with the slogan:

'When you wish upon a star …
You're a few million light years late.
That star is dead.
JUST LIKE YOUR DREAMS.'

PERHAPS IMAGINING herself the subject of a rousing movie about a failing student made good by the patient attentions of an inspirational teacher, a Florida teacher did indeed instil a young boy with the confidence to enter a public speaking competition – but she was roundly criticized for the content of his speech, which singled out and disparaged a former teacher at the school.

The speech, entitled 'My Bad Teacher' and later described by the defendant as 'a ten-year-old's speech for ten-year-olds', was effectively a rant against the former teacher's laziness, forgetfulness and impatience. It might well have stayed within the four walls of the assembly hall had one of the ten-year-olds in attendance not been the former teacher's own child, who was not best pleased at hearing his mother publicly excoriated as 'the worst teacher ever'.

THE PRINCIPAL of a school in Dallas raised serious concerns about his suitability for the job when it emerged in 2009 that he had sanctioned cage fights between feuding students.

The former police officer, already in many parents' bad books for lying about being kidnapped and mugged in order to get paid leave and also for his part in a grade-altering scandal, allowed and apparently encouraged the bare-knuckle fights in a caged-off area of the boys' changing room. He even provided security guards to watch over the youths, instructing them to 'let them duke it out'.

When solicited by journalists for his opinion on the matter, a professor at Indiana University's the Safe and Responsive Schools Project made the needless comment that 'those types of strategies just don't work.'

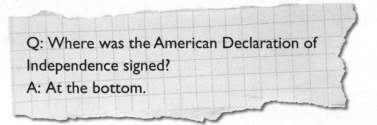

Q: Where was the American Declaration of Independence signed?
A: At the bottom.

EXPERIMENTAL TEACHING

TEACHERS THE world over are usually praised for coming up with cross-subject exercises that combine key educational topics from across the curriculum. Not so for Jane Youn, a maths teacher at Manhattan's Public School 59, who, in January 2013, decided to introduce elements of her students' history lessons into their arithmetic homework, which included the following questions:

1. In a slave ship, there can be 3,799 slaves. One day, the slaves took over the ship. 1,897 are dead. How many slaves are alive?
2. One slave got whipped five times a day. How many times did he get whipped in a month (31 days)? Another slave got whipped nine times a day. How many times did he get whipped in a month? How many times did the two slaves get whipped together in one month?

Incredibly, this was not an isolated moment of madness. In 2011, at Beaver Ridge Elementary School in Norcross, Georgia, another maths teacher had had a similar spark of inspiration...

1. Each tree had 56 oranges. If eight slaves pick them equally, then how much would each slave pick?

2. If Frederick got two beatings per day, how many beatings did he get in one week?

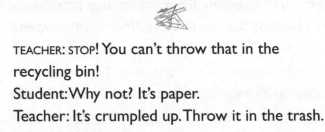

TEACHER: STOP! You can't throw that in the recycling bin!
Student: Why not? It's paper.
Teacher: It's crumpled up. Throw it in the trash.

AN ILLINOIS social studies teacher was surprised to be reprimanded by school authorities after he taught his students about the Fifth Amendment – the right not to incriminate oneself – although admittedly he might have chosen his moment better. The school had asked teachers to circulate a survey asking frank questions about students' use of alcohol and drugs, and upon realizing the questionnaire was not anonymous this particular teacher had reminded his charges they needn't implicate themselves in any extracurricular wrongdoing.

The teacher defended his actions, saying he would have taken issue with the survey sooner had he seen it, but that he had acted spontaneously because 'there was no time to ask anyone'. The students perhaps understandably organized a 5,000-strong petition urging school authorities not to sack their new favourite teacher, although the man at the centre of the case remained remarkably relaxed.

'I'm not a martyr,' he told reporters. 'Calm down.'

A SCHOOL in Florida caused widespread upset and a misguided understanding of world history when it surprised its students one morning in 2006 with a Holocaust reenactment exercise.

Upon arrival at the school, pupils whose surnames fell in the second half of the alphabet were issued Star of David clothing badges like those forced upon Jews by the Nazis, and told they had no right to use certain school facilities. One child 'was forced to go to the back of the lunch line four times by an administrator' and was made to stand during all his lessons. He went home in tears, saying 'The only thing I found out today is that I don't want to be Jewish.'

The school principal stood by the spirit of the exercise, if not necessarily its execution, explaining, 'Teachers felt that it would have defeated the purpose to tell the students ahead of time because that would have prepared them.'

In a commendably diplomatic response to the ill-thought-out incident, Florida's Holocaust Memorial

Resource and Education Center issued a statement 'applauding the school's effort to engage in Holocaust education with the hope of a tolerance education component in the classroom' but emphasizing that it did not 'encourage teachers to engage in simulation exercises'.

SOCIAL STUDIES students at a school in New York were at first intrigued by their teacher's announcement that she would enliven a class on slavery through role-play. But it became clear, by the time two thirteen-year-old girls found themselves crouching under a desk with their hands and feet tied together with tape, that the exercise had – in the words of the director of the local branch of the National Association for the Advancement of Colored People – 'gone wrong'.

'We don't want to discourage creativity,' the school's superintendent commented afterwards, although he promised to undertake 'conversations with staff on how to deliver effective lessons'.

A TEACHER in Florida took the notion of 'being cruel to be kind' rather too far one day when she killed the class pets using a shovel. Elementary school teacher Jane Bender explained to the children that the baby rabbits had been rejected by their mother and would suffer as a consequence, but then tried to convince them that the bunnies ought simply to be buried alive. When the children understandably refused, Bender grabbed the shovel and dispatched them herself – right in front of the children.

When Animal Services were called in to investigate, the teacher conceded that she had 'made a bad decision'.

THE PRINCIPAL of a high school in Minnesota was left with some explaining to do after overseeing a bizarre event in which blindfolded students were tricked into 'making out' with their own parents.

Having been told they would be kissed by 'a special someone' – most likely, or so they thought, a fellow student – the captains of the school's sports teams were lined up on stage and blindfolded before being approached and passionately kissed by their non-blindfolded mother or father.

After videos of the event went viral in 2011, accompanied by a great deal of criticism, one parent commented: 'I think people need to have more of a sense of humor!'

Q: Name six animals that live in the Arctic.
A: Two polar bears and four seals.

TEACHERS WHO accompanied a group of Canadian high school students on a field trip in 2012 had to be disciplined on their return after it emerged they had tricked the students into eating moose droppings.

The teachers from Walter Whyte School in Manitoba – including the school principal – presented the children with what they claimed were chocolate-covered almonds, and everyone enthusiastically tucked in. It was only then that the teachers revealed 'You just ate moose shit!' and burst out laughing. One girl got the faeces stuck in her braces and vomited, and she and another student ended up having to be taken to hospital.

While a number of parents refused to send their children back to school following the disastrous field trip, the school superintendent summed the situation up quite neatly when he called it 'a very poorly conceived joke'.

A SCHOOL in Mississippi was accused of being stuck in the dark ages in 2010 when it emerged that certain positions on the student council were reserved for people of a specific race.

The school in Nettleton had originally instituted the racial stipulations in an attempt at positive discrimination in the 1970s – but then not altered the policy for over thirty years. It only came to light when a mixed-race girl was informed she didn't qualify for any of the positions because she wasn't black or white.

Pity the students of the smart-Alec teacher who set this unusual three-minute test:
1. Read everything before you do anything.
2. Put your name in the upper right-hand corner of this page.
3. Circle the word 'name' in sentence two.
4. Draw five small squares in the top right-hand corner under your name.
5. Put an X in each square you have just drawn.
6. Put a circle around each square.
7. Sign your name under the title of this page.

8. After the title write 'yes yes yes'.
9. Underline sentences number seven and eight.
10. Put an X in the lower left-hand corner of this page.
11. Draw a triangle around the X you have just made.
12. On the back of this page multiply seven by thirty.
13. Draw a circle around the word 'top' on sentence four.
14. Loudly call out your first name when you reach this point in the test.
15. If you think you have carefully followed these directions, tell a partner 'I have carefully followed the directions.'
16. On the reverse side of this paper add 107 and 278.
17. Count out in your normal speaking voice from one to ten.
18. If you are the first person to get this far, write your name on the board.
19. Punch three small holes in your paper with your pencil here ...
20. Now that you have finished reading carefully, do only numbers one and two.

BIOLOGY TEACHER: Eskimos can survive without vegetables because they eat lots of polar bears and penguins.

Students: But penguins and polar bears don't live at the same poles.

Teacher: Well … obviously I meant the South Pole. Eskimos eat the penguins.

Students: What?

FOR A number of months in 2012, Suzy Harriston was one of the most popular girls at Clayton High School, Missouri. She had 300 friends on Facebook, all of them fellow students, and was a regular presence on the social networking site. But nobody could recall seeing her in class. It took a particularly eagle-eyed student to notice that there was no Suzy Harriston at the school, and that the profile was in fact a front for the principal, Louise Losos.

After the aggrieved student posted his theory on Facebook, Suzy mysteriously disappeared. The following day, Principal Losos did likewise.

Q: Kazakhstan is home to many nice people, including Borat. The first person to stand and, in your best Borat voice, say 'I am Borat. I like you. Very nice!' will receive a bonus point.

ORDER, ORDER!

WHAT GOES AROUND comes around... The polite pupils of a young but dragon-like technology teacher in Birmingham sat through an entire class without telling her her skirt was tucked into her tights, for fear of her venomous tongue.

A SIX-year-old boy accused of bullying at a kindergarten in Texas had a life lesson well and truly drilled into him when two teachers orchestrated a punishment in which twenty-four of his classmates lined up and hit him.

According to police, the incident was designed

to show the child 'why bullying is bad', although the image of two teachers goading twenty-four children to 'Hit him! Hit him harder!' may seem at odds with the message it was intended to convey. Nonetheless, the infants got well and truly into the spirit of things, the boy's mother later reporting that 'most of them hit him twice'.

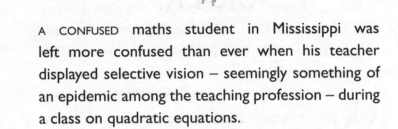

A CONFUSED maths student in Mississippi was left more confused than ever when his teacher displayed selective vision – seemingly something of an epidemic among the teaching profession – during a class on quadratic equations.

'I raised my hand to ask for clarification,' he explains. 'The teacher kept teaching and ignored me for a solid five minutes – looking directly at me more than once – and had moved on to something else by the time he finally asked me what I had my hand up for. When I asked my question he told me I should have asked it five minutes earlier when we were still on that topic. He refused to answer my question.'

A NEWLY qualified geography teacher had the wool pulled over his eyes by the class bullies after they locked eight of their fellow students in the bag cupboard at the back of the room. Claiming that the missing students had been held back by another teacher and would arrive shortly, the grinning girls challenged him to a board game to pass the time while they waited.

'The poor guy,' one student commented years later. 'Half the class was suffocating in the bag cupboard while he naïvely played Boggle with the perpetrators.'

A UNIVERSITY professor became an unexpected YouTube sensation in 2006 thanks to his reaction to a student taking a phone call during a lecture. Without interrupting his introductory comments to the class, the teacher walked over to the distracted student, smilingly held out his hand for the phone, and then smashed it to the ground – all while continuing his monologue.

AN ELEMENTARY teacher in Louisiana gave one of her young pupils a dubious lesson in taking responsibility for one's actions when she insisted he unblock the toilet he had accidentally put out of action – using his bare hands.

Seven-year-old Trevor was understandably embarrassed to admit he had 'made the toilet overflow with toilet paper and poo', but wasn't quite expecting Ms Landry to dole out such a Dickensian punishment.

It gets worse, according to the boy's mother, who claimed that the teacher – who was sacked for her actions in 2008 – 'told him next time, if you do it again, she gonna make him pull it out with his teeth'.

WHILE DETENTION is a punishment normally reserved for serious misdemeanours on school property, some teachers seem to have a particularly low tolerance threshold, as these comments on detention slips by teachers in the United States show:

- 'After a student said "Can it be that big?" (innocent comment) he responded "That's what she said."'
- 'He stood up and unbuttoned his shirt to

reveal a Superman T-shirt, and then announced that he was Superman.'
• 'Calling a teacher a "muggle".'

AN ELEMENTARY school teacher in Tennessee, fed up with one child's persistent messiness, devised a memorable punishment when she corralled the other pupils into surrounding the culprit and making pig noises at him.

'Your area looks like a pig sty,' Debbie Hayes had told the infant, adding: 'Oink. Oink.' When a fellow teacher happened to wander into the room a few moments later she found the whole class 'making pig sounds' at the unfortunate child.

Meanwhile, over in Georgia, a teacher sorely regretted giving one child the 'Bermuda Triangle Award' – for a messy desk she lightheartedly described as 'the place where things go in but never come back out' – after the child burst into tears and had to be taken home.

AN ASSISTANT principal in North Carolina took discipline a step or three too far during the hunt for some stolen money, when he insisted on strip-searching an eight-year-old boy.

The boy had found a $20 bill on the floor and given it back to the girl who had dropped it, but when she subsequently mislaid the money again the eye of suspicion fell on to the do-gooder. The assistant principal demanded the boy strip down to his underwear to prove that he didn't have the money, which was shortly thereafter found under a table in the cafeteria.

Q: Brian has 50 slices of cake. He eats 48.
What has he now?
A: Diabetes. Brian has fuckin' diabetes.

A YOUNG English teacher struggling to maintain order in a class of wayward twelve-year-old boys was cheered up, albeit temporarily, when the head of the English department and his deputy burst out of the book cupboard wearing garish wigs and singing show tunes.

'I have no idea what they were doing in there,' she commented, 'but it certainly changed the tone of the lesson!'

A TEACHER of modern languages who was all too used to xenophobic abuse from her disobedient pupils hit on the perfect riposte to the age-old question 'Why don't you just f**k off to where you came from?'

Turning to the smug bully in question, she smiled politely and asked: 'Why don't you just go and play on the motorway?'

Q: Write a sentence using the word 'facetious'.
A: This sentence uses the word 'facetious'.

TWO TEACHERS in Texas, apparently taking inspiration from a book about monsters they were reading in class, unwittingly managed to give their students lifelong nightmares by locking them in what they called 'the monster cupboard'. The case came to a head when a four-year-old laughed at his classmate for being thrown in the pitch-black cupboard and wound up in there himself, ultimately becoming so terrified that he felt unwell and had to be sent home.

'There was a monster and the monster was going to eat me,' the poor child later reported.

A SCIENCE teacher in Florida thought she had come up with an amusing way to keep her students on the straight and narrow in class: anyone who misbehaved would be forced to don 'the cone of shame' – a cone collar normally reserved for injured dogs. Minor infractions such as eating and drinking in class were apparently enough to warrant this treatment, which the students by all accounts found rather amusing.

Their parents, alas, did not – especially when photos of the unusual form of punishment somehow found their way onto Facebook.

'That's a human, not an animal,' said one. 'I was disgusted – very disgusted.'

Following the outcry that accompanied the publication of the photos, the teacher in question admitted that making her students wear dog collars had 'probably' been a bad idea.

THERE WERE awkward looks all round during a university English literature lecture when the meek-mannered professor, discussing Douglas Adams' *The Hitchhiker's Guide to the Galaxy*, repeatedly referred to the fictional computer Deep Thought as Deep Throat.

A CAUTIONARY tale for any teacher who's ever struggled to gain a class's attention: police were called to a school in Atherton, California in March 2011 after a pupil dialled 911 to report that her maths teacher was 'causing a disturbance'. He had rattled her desk to make her pay attention and she had apparently been startled by the noise.

By the time police arrived the incident had been all but forgotten and the lesson was continuing as planned, but the fact that they had attended the scene at all gave the school's superintendent no option but to put the teacher on paid leave.

AN IMPATIENT teacher in Russia got a retort he wasn't expecting after he berated a young girl for her ignorance during an English class. Having picked on her in front of her friends and gone so far as to start jabbing at her head, the teacher was rounded on by the child, who swatted his arm away and then kicked him in the testicles. Unfortunately the whole incident was captured on video and posted to YouTube, after which the teacher was suspended for his 'aggressive teaching'.

Q: What were the circumstances of John F.
Kennedy's death?
A: Suspicious.

MATHS TEACHERS must be used to their pupils nodding off mid-class, but one enterprising professor in New York got his own back on a snoozing student by crawling under the desks and tying the boy's shoelaces together.

THE PARENTS of a disruptive pupil facing expulsion for throwing a ball of paper at his economics teacher found themselves in a moral quandary after the teacher offered to keep his mouth shut in return for €10,000.

The details of the alleged extortion, which took place in northern France in 2011 and 2012, vary widely between one party and the other, but what is not in doubt is that the teacher had a financial agreement drawn up, which the boy's father signed, and that monthly payments of €300 subsequently started making their way to the teacher's bank account. The boy was not expelled...

...until January 2013, for an unrelated incident, at which point his father finally felt able to reveal the underhand financial arrangement. In something of an understatement, the French minister for education commented that extortion was 'a serious contravention of the values of public educational service' that the teacher was meant to espouse.

AFTER ONE too many facetious interruptions during her English class, an enraged teacher rounded on the troublemaker: 'That's it! I've had enough. I'm going to call your father when I'm off my period' – confused faces – 'I mean when I'm off *next* period!' The rest of the lesson was a write-off.

WHEN A diminutive Spanish-language teacher tripped over an enormous schoolbag and fell flat on her face mid-lesson – again – she decided enough was enough and began berating the student nearest the bag.

'But it ain't mine!' protested the student.

'You can't pull the sheeps over my eyes!' was the quick-fire retort.

NORMALLY MINDFUL of using age-appropriate language in front of her students, one teacher suffered a malfunction of her self-censoring mechanism when she complained to another, in front of a class, that she had been 'running around like a blue-arsed dot-dot-dot'.

Q: What did Mahatma Gandhi and Genghis Khan have in common?
A: Unusual names.

AN ENGLISH teacher who clearly adhered strictly to the working hours set out in her contract of employment made sure students were aware of her schedule by posting this helpful notice on her classroom wall: 'My emergency paper reader is Helen Waite. If you think that your paper must be read immediately, go to Helen Waite.'

EVERY PARENT will recognize the scenario: you dutifully show up at your child's school fete and need to be seen to be supportive, so end up buying forty tickets for the tombola or overbidding on some ridiculously useless item in the attic-junk auction. For one charitably minded couple in a wealthy part of Manhattan, however, the stakes ended up being astronomically higher than they could ever have imagined.

The parents in question were unable to attend the benefit evening at their children's expensive school on the Upper East Side, but, in an arguably foolhardy show of generosity, had instructed a third party to outbid everyone during the auction of a unique painting. The unique thing about the painting being that it had been executed by a number of the schoolchildren themselves, including the couple's own son. Having imagined they might be called upon to fork out a couple of thousand dollars, the parents were incredulous to discover they had unwittingly offered $50,000 for the artwork, thanks to one of the school's own teachers refusing to drop out of the bidding.

Convinced that the teachers had rigged the auction, the parents sued the school for $415,900 in June 2013, seeking recompense not only for the world's most expensive collage but also for the cost of relocating their children to a new school and hiring a chauffeur to transport them there.

BIBLIOGRAPHY

Richard Benson, *F in Exams* (Summersdale Publishers, 2008)

Anna Tripp, *School Fail: Hilarious Howlers from School* (Michael O'Mara Books Ltd, 2011)

www.cracked.com

www.dailymail.co.uk

www.gawker.com

www.guardian.co.uk

www.huffingtonpost.co.uk

www.leparisien.fr

www.reddit.com

www.snopes.com

www.studentbeans.com

www.telegraph.co.uk

www.thelocal.fr

www.twitter.com

IF YOU ENJOYED *BAD TEACHER,* YOU'LL LOVE

The Sunday Times Bestseller by Wendy Roby

ISBN 978-1-84317-466-0
in paperback print format

ISBN 978-1-84317-618-3
in ePub format

ISBN 978-1-84317-619-0
in Mobipocket format

By Anna Trip

ISBN 978-1-84317-689-3
in paperback print format

ISBN 978-1-84317-819-4
in ePub format

ISBN 978-1-84317-820-0
in Mobipocket format